CONCEPTUALIZING 2000

PROACTIVE

PLANNING

CONCEPTUALIZING 2000

PROACTIVE

75957

PLANNING

Dan Angel
and Mike DeVault,
Editors

THE COMMUNITY COLLEGE PRESS
A DIVISION OF THE AMERICAN ASSOCIATION OF
COMMUNITY AND JUNIOR COLLEGES

Published by The Community College Press, a division of the American Association
of Community and Junior Colleges
National Center for Higher Education
One Dupont Circle, N.W., Suite 410
Washington, D.C. 20036
Phone: (202) 728-0200

ISBN: 0-87117-226-7
Library of Congress Catalog Card Number: 91-70258

To Pat, Scott, and Shelby
—D.A.

My efforts on this book are dedicated to my dad,
who passed away in December 1990
—M.D.

PART ONE: THE PLANNING CONTEXT

Part Two: The Issues

COLLEGE PLANNING AND goal-setting sessions have been called the "sauna bath" of higher education. With ideas and the creative juices flowing freely, our "problems" become "challenges," and once impossible solutions appear right under our noses. In the throes of planning, the enthusiasm that is generated makes us feel warm all over. Then we emerge from the planning process with a shiny, crisp document full of good ideas—and face the cold, cruel world of everyday problems. However well-intentioned plans are, sometimes the only useful function they ultimately serve is holding up a row of books on a bookshelf . . . and the life of the college does not change much.

The editors of *Conceptualizing 2000* know that in this era of rapid change, it's time to think of planning in the context of action—that a plan without an action component is little more than a sauna bath. As we race toward the year 2000, our success or failure will hinge on thoughtful planning backed up by the actions we take today.

There are exciting, as well as challenging, times ahead for community, technical, and junior college leaders. The community college mission will become increasingly complex as the communities and students we serve expect more and more from us. In the future, they will turn to us more than ever to provide affordable higher education, job training and retraining, community service, and opportunity to move into the economic mainstream of American life.

Against the backdrop of these challenges, Dan Angel and Mike DeVault have assembled an impressive cast of experts to discuss planning's new dimensions. Some discuss components of the planning process—creating visions, renewing the institution, scanning the environment, building linkages. Others explore the basic planning issues of growing student diversity, accountability pressures, and new definitions of effectiveness, assessment, and success.

Among them, the contributing writers to this volume have hundreds of years of experience leading dozens of community, technical, and junior colleges. They have faced the issues. They are successful because of their ability to plan strategically, putting their institutions in a position to move beyond reaction and become proactive, often moving beyond the immediate problem into a whole new plane of operations. We will do well to heed their lessons and advice.

Whether we stand still and let the world change around us, or plan for the year 2000 by meeting our challenges head-on, will mean the difference between stagnating institutions and fulfilling our mission as America's colleges of opportunity.

—Dale Parnell
President
AACJC

CONCEPTUALIZING 2000: PROACTIVE PLANNING is written by a number of national community college leaders. Its purpose is to convey the needs of the decade ahead and to sketch a new framework for planning—and action. As the writers who have contributed their talents clearly tell us, it is time for new approaches. This book presents a broad range of action-oriented responses to the challenges that lie ahead. Conceptualizing 2000 does not offer a generic guide to an anticipated future, but rather a working handbook for the American community college in the unpredictable 1990s. Whether the ancient Chinese dictum, "May you live in interesting times," will be a blessing or a curse depends on the determination and ingenuity of your leadership and your institution.

Part One of the book sets the stage for the planning process. The authors discuss the dynamics of planning and offer models carefully crafted for the times ahead.

As institutions reach different stages of organizational growth, new and more complex expectations are placed on them. Chapter 1 introduces a new planning model to help institutions respond.

Chapter 2 argues that planning must attempt to achieve a distinguished level; otherwise internal drains on energy and external constraints will be counterproductive. In Chapter 3, planning is described as a deliberate decision to change and improve. Chapter 4 examines what it will take for community colleges to achieve renewal not only for themselves, but also for the communities they serve.

Dramatic future change presents multifaceted opportunities for proactive planning; Chapter 5 maintains that we must unlock the genius and creativity of our faculty, staff, and institutional leaders.

Our institutions have to present an image that is responsible and successful. In other words, as argued in Chapter 6, things have to get done—issues must be addressed responsibly and solutions must be found and implemented.

Chapter 7 explores the idea of partnerships as a proven tool for creative solutions. The importance of collaboration within the institution and how to energize our collective talents for problem solving is pursued in Chapter 8. Chapter 9 reminds us that without the necessary financial resources, many new initiatives will never be implemented.

Because planning is often imposed from an external source, Chapter 10 offers valuable lessons from a statewide planning effort in Kentucky.

With the context for planning thus outlined, the second half of the book turns to some of the emerging issues facing community colleges in the future. These are the conditions, trends, and challenges that we must plan *for*.

Chapter 11 focuses attention on a number of national issues that will require local solutions: 10,000 children a year lost to poverty; thirty-five million people over age sixty-five by the year 2000; twenty-three million people who are functionally illiterate; and a national school drop-out rate of 26 percent.

Two chapters are directed to the most compelling issue in higher education today. Whether it is called "Equality of Opportunity," "Access to Higher Education," or "Access and Success," a similar message is sounded: the idea of building opportunity for those who have traditionally been denied it. Chapters 12 and 13 articulate this key planning issue.

Institutional effectiveness is another issue that must increasingly draw our attention in the future. Chapter 14 directs our focus to the fact that any discussion of effectiveness must consider the wide range of different—and seemingly competing—missions of community colleges.

Chapter 15 examines the need for faculty and administrative renewal. The opportunities to solve the major issues of our day will be improved only when our institutions participate fully and enthusiastically in building better communities.

The road to quality will likely be unfulfilled if our decisions are based on conventional wisdom and not solid research. Chapter 16 explains the need for good data. The plight of urban America and the necessity for a major initiative to solve urban problems is defined in Chapter 17.

The expanding meaning of the term "community" is presented in Chapter 18. The future community must include a global base as an integral part of the community college mission. Chapter 19 provides valuable insights into the role of technology in helping colleges adapt to the diversity of learners and learning styles.

We hope this book will serve as a bridge—one that spans the best ideas of earlier planning models with the creative new ideas needed to move us toward a new generation of proactive planning.

We have it within our means as America's community college network to forge a new future within each community, our nation, and our world. As we conceptualize the future and work proactively, we are building America one community at a time.

Dan Angel
Mike DeVault
Austin, Texas
November 1, 1990

THE
PLANNING
CONTEXT

CHAPTER ONE

Proactive Planning: A Fourth-Generation Approach

By Dan Angel and Mike DeVault

A NY DOUBTING THOMAS of the need for planning could profit from the three modern graces of gaffe: the Original, Space Age, and Governmental Finance.

The Original: In April 1985 Coca-Cola management made an Edsel-like decision. Original-formula Coke—America's number-one selling soft drink—was replaced by a new, sweeter-tasting formula. The decision was so unpopular that within 100 days the ensuing consumer revolt persuaded the top brass at Coke to put another decision on the shelf. Instead of pulling the new formula from the market, the management proclaimed that the original Coca-Cola Classic would share consumer favors with New Coke.

Five years later, the full magnitude of the blunder was evident. Original-formula Coke was still America's top-selling soft drink, with 20 percent of the market. New Coke? Just over a 1 percent share.

Space Age: In April 1990 the much anticipated and ballyhooed Hubble Telescope was launched from the space shuttle Discovery. Although it was touted as the most sophisticated scientific instrument ever built (sounds Titanic, doesn't it?), there were instantaneous problems. The 100-inch primary mirror was unable to focus light from distant stars as anticipated. NASA experts later announced that the mirror on this $1.5 billion instrument had been built precisely—precisely wrong.

Scientists hope to correct this defect during a space mission—in 1993!

Governmental Finance: Back in 1985 Congress enacted the Gramm-Rudman-Hollings Act, which mandated that Congress and the President work toward a balanced budget by setting predetermined annual deficit targets. If an agreement cannot be reached by the start of a new fiscal year, large across-the-board spending cuts are automatically actuated.

In the five years since the deficit reduction law passed, the federal deficit has gone up $1.4 trillion.

The History of Planning

The need for effective planning is obvious, yet planning is certainly not a new concept. In formulating new ideas about planning, we must first look back across the generations and take our cue from the volumes of earlier writings and theories.

In the Frederick Taylor concept of traditional management, organizations were advised to structure themselves around five concepts: planning, organizing, commanding, controlling, and coordinating. While commanding and controlling in the classic sense have generally vanished from contemporary management, planning continues to be an essential part of organizational life.

Planning was, and continues to be, the formulation of a program of action designed to achieve a specific end. When planning is examined across the generations, three distinctive eras can be observed.

The first generation of planning was a method of bringing order to an organization's efforts. It was a systematic way of controlling the internal environment while maximizing external results. Planning was generally engaged in only by those in top management, and the resulting plan flowed downward to those who would help implement it. Planning was reactive instead of adaptive. It brought a necessary order and consistency to important organizational goals. It provided a means to keep everyone in lock-step toward a specific target. Organizations were much more autocratic, and aligning the organization's planning goals with those who worked to fulfill them was relatively easy. When everyone accepts planning goals, regardless of how they have been set, organizational movement toward planning targets is more likely to occur. This was the nature of organizations during the classical period—planning's first generation.

The basic ideas about planning stayed relatively unchanged until the introduction of long-range planning. This second-generation approach introduced the idea that planning could not be done just for the short term, but needed to serve as a guide over time for the organization's future direction.

The Industrial Revolution brought about many organizational changes, among them the emergence of a substantial number of large, complex organizations. As organizations became more complex, long-range planning stressed the importance of time linkages, which is the idea that programs and activities pursued today have a relationship to those that can be pursued tomorrow. The achievement of a specific end as described in the original concept of planning became multiple ends that were inextricably connected.

With the third generation came the concept of strategic planning. What marked this planning design was an emphasis on the conditions external to the organization that affect the organization's pursuit of attainable goals. Strategic planning fosters adaptation. It requires institutions to define what they can and cannot do.

During planning's first two generations, organizations were viewed as closed. From Taylor to Henri Fayol to Max Weber, and even through the human relations period, organizations viewed themselves as inside-out operations. If they could be controlled on the inside, then outside goals were easily achievable.

Because we now know organizations are open systems, they all must, in order to survive, give something to the environment and receive something in exchange. Strategic long-range planning also focused attention on the obvious interrelationships between the organization and the organizations external to it, both formal and informal.

In the traditional scheme of management theory, power was considered to be the capacity to marshall the resources needed to accomplish a given task or achieve a specific goal. Strategic planning recognized a power relationship that comes from dependency. Organizations depend on a network of other organizations for support, and, in turn, these other organizations depend on the focal organization for some output. Dependency is the reverse way of stating a power relationship. Strategic planning recognizes this power relationship and requires planners to understand the dynamic nature of this relationship.

Strategic planning's concepts of an open system, external environment, and dependency were basically ignored in earlier planning models, since a planning model generally reflects the needs of the time. In the early days of the modern management era, organizations were generally independent. They were not required to satisfy diverse external groups, and planning was a simpler process. As the number of variables in the planning process increases, the consideration of interactions and interdependencies becomes much more complex.

Adaptability or Reaction?

There have been times when the capacity to simply react to given circumstances has been sufficient to meet specific goals and address existing needs. There have been times when change has occurred slowly. When change is slow, organizations generally have the luxury of time in which to alter systems and respond. But external change has taken on the fast-paced characteristics of other facets of the late twentieth century. Recognition of the inevitability of change and the ability to meet its challenges are the foundations for assessing and improving the planning system. Today an organization's reliance on reactive planning will quickly render it unproductive. Organizations must improve their planning systems to focus more externally and create an institutional/environmental fit. When the institution and the environment have some degree of congruity, the goal of adaptive planning has been reached.

Building an institutional planning process is no small task. It requires time, energy, resources, and unswerving commitment throughout the institution. Dwight Eisenhower said that "the process of planning is everything and that the plan itself is nothing." Today both the process and product are critical.

Planning must become the formulation of a program of action designed to achieve specific ends. Planners must also acknowledge the rapid change inherent in an information age; organizations will have less time to adapt to changing environments. Time will be substantially reduced and the nature of planning permanently altered.

Reaction, the consistent element throughout the earlier stages of planning, will no longer provide an acceptable response to complex and dynamic issues.

5

Planning must continue to be organized around an open system that acknowledges the external environment and the dependent relationship between it and the institution. The notion that organizations must satisfy a diverse group of external interests in exchange for their support is so important that many have concluded that the ultimate measure of an organization's effectiveness is simply the degree to which it has satisfied its many constituents.

Those who lead or participate in an institutional planning process must be actively involved, flexible, and alert to environmental changes. They also must be willing to take action.

While planning must continue to be the formulation of a program of action designed to achieve certain goals, it must also accommodate anticipated change. Planning will require leadership that is visionary and futuristic. Future planning efforts must include qualities that have been neglected or unnecessary in earlier models, such as an expectation, a commitment, and a call to action.

When considering the major issues pursued in this book, any planning process that concludes without a commitment to action will be a planning process that hasn't achieved its full potential. When organizations plan, they must plan to act.

Square Peg in a Round Hole

The three stages of organizational growth have frequently been described as birth, youth, and maturity. Most of the nation's community, junior, and technical colleges have reached the last stage. A critical concern for any organization at this stage is to contribute to society. If it does not, it will find a lack of public respect and appreciation. Our colleges are being reshaped in response to major issues, such as access, quality, and equity. Our institutions must respond or fail. It is that simple!

Everyone is familiar with the expression, "You can't put a square peg into a round hole." We all know that putting the round peg into the round hole is easy. It is putting the square peg into the round hole that gets complicated.

Community colleges have long been a beacon of hope for a new generation of college students who have arrived in many different sizes and shapes. There are those who would consider the efforts of the community colleges in serving this student diversity somewhat akin to the square peg/round hole dilemma. While some community, technical, and junior colleges have been successful in proving this expression wrong, that success will be increasingly difficult to sustain unless we plan more effectively and take appropriate action. The environmental dynamics are too complex to do otherwise in a nation where one out of every three people will be non-White soon after the year 2000.

A comprehensive planning approach that anticipates environmental changes will make a substantial difference in a college's level of success. Other issues, including declining enrollments, shrinking financial resources, and mounting pressures for accountability, undoubtedly have contributed to this new interest in planning. Attention to demographic and enrollment forecasting, academic programming, student services, improved retention, and human resource planning for academic staff are among the issues facing community colleges from within.

In addition, major issues brought about by technological advances, legal changes, and societal developments such as diversity in higher education, technology expansion, civic responsibility, an aging population, global understanding, cultural awareness, urban decay, and underpreparedness of entering students compound the planning process.

So, faced with square pegs and round holes, community colleges have three options: (1) change the type of peg (student); (2) stretch the hole grudgingly (the institution); or (3) create a new, receptive structure. Changing the peg (people) cannot be the answer. We have to take people as they are. Option two, an unwilling compliance, is doomed to failure.

Option three is the only workable solution if we aim to actually accommodate the peg (our students). In other words, planners need to anticipate that square pegs are coming and that the present system accommodates round ones. To the extent that this anticipation occurs, the organization's effectiveness will be measured positively by external groups. The ability of an organization to cause society to give it freedom to continue meeting challenges and continue to be innovative in its services will depend on the ability to continually reshape and renew our institutions.

The community college has always had a unique place in the mosaic of American higher education. Our challenge has been both difficult and significant. Yet, the substantive challenges before us today are even greater, and the capacity for even greater levels of success must be found. Planning for greatness has to be our first priority. We will not reach a level of greatness by accident.

Proactive Planning: A Fourth-Generation Approach

Planning, as a process, is more complex today than in generations past. It must embrace and foster new dimensions. Planning has never been a simple exercise, and it is likely to become more complex as society evolves and changes the products and systems we depend on.

Each generation is marked by constructive (adaptive) changes to these products and systems. We need not look any further than the development of computers to observe significant changes from one generation to the next. As computers have driven themselves to change, so must institutions and institutional planners.

A nineteenth-century mathematician named Charles Babbage developed the first computing machine. Even though it was a simple mechanical object, it showed his contemporaries the basic idea of a computer. Lord Byron's niece, Ada Lovelace, gave us the first recorded logic sequence through instructions to her maid. Number theory and cryptography came together during World War II as Americans tried to break the German Enigma Code. Each of these events helped set the stage for the modern computer.

In the late 1940s, Univac introduced the first commercial computer, transistors replaced vacuum tubes as bytes of memory and large mainframe systems evolved. From the late '40s to the mid-'70s, computers conjured up notions of small rooms, gadgeteers in white coats, and many flashing lights. The next generation brought the personal computer and computer networks. Future generations will bring even smaller and faster machines, each one farther away from Babbage's "computing machine."

As we move toward a new century, unparalleled, accelerated change will continue to be the norm. Technology is moving faster than schools can keep pace and, as a result, the U.S. Congress is planning to import the technological expertise America seems unable to produce. Our inability to produce technological expertise might be linked to the inability to plan for the changes that are occurring.

Institutions need to move farther away from earlier, simpler models of planning structures that respond to the organizational and societal complexities of the late twentieth century. To organize planning as it was done in earlier generations will be ineffective for organizations, the individuals, and the communities that depend on them.

It is time to elevate the planning process to another level of improvement. It is time to incorporate the best characteristics of earlier planning with new dimensions that will improve the planning process. It is time for planning's fourth generation.

Fourth-generation planning—proactive planning—is value-based, action-oriented planning that adds needed new urgency to the planning process. To the extent that institutions are able to meet the challenges of these new dimensions, they will move closer to achieving success in meeting the challenges of our time.

For planning to be proactive, it must
- be conceptual
- recognize environmental conditions
- anticipate and accommodate rapid change
- recognize dependency
- be inclusive
- be an open process
- include a call to action
- help institutions reach a level of distinction
- change the institutional culture
- be value-based

- be adaptive

Each dimension requires planners and plans to meet certain conditions. Proactive planning is conceptual when institutions are able to see and understand as much of the whole picture as they can before attempting to design a plan to address issues and set priorities. In planning, like other activities, the whole is greater than the sum of its often narrowly vested parts. Conceptualizing keeps institutions from censoring dreams and limiting visions. Conceptualizing allows planners to dream big dreams. Conceptual planning requires a general concept, outlined before specific planning begins, of the broad parameters that should help define the planning process.

As demographic, economic, educational, cultural, and social trends change simultaneously with increasing accountability pressures, institutions must be able to respond to external expectations. Planners who do not understand what is going on around them will produce a plan that is useless in moving the institution forward. Proactive planning recognizes the environmental conditions that help frame the planning process and adopts strategic operational priorities that respond effectively.

A planning process that ignores the accelerated nature of our world is likely to produce an end product that is useful for only a limited period of time. Proactive planning anticipates and accommodates rapid change because as institutions and as individuals we are traveling on the fast track. This is the contingency nature of planning—to develop a product that has utility beyond a finite amount of time. The contingency dimension of planning allows institutions to change as market conditions change.

People make institutions in the same way as they make communities and societies. In a sense, organizations depend on people for output, and people are dependent on organizations for output. This power relationship rests on the idea of dependency. Proactive planning recognizes the dependency between the institution and its environment. This promotes the opportunity to fashion a planning process and product that unite organizational goals and people.

Proactive planning is inclusive through the involvement of both those who must carry out the initiatives described by the plan and those who will depend on the plan for an improved quality of life and a better and more responsive community.

Proactive planning is an open process that allows for participation by the many instead of the few and that is void of hidden agendas, predetermined outcomes that the planning process is intended only to validate, and parochial interests. Planning is an open process when the plan is not relegated to the bookshelf but lives in college budgets and throughout operational priorities.

Peter Drucker suggested that "if you do not have a plan for the future, you will have no future." In the same way, a plan without an action requirement is no plan at all. Proactive planning includes a call to action by clearly defining who will be responsible for the goals of the plan, what they will do to move the institution toward these goals, in what time frame they will do so, the accountability measures that will be used to ensure outcome success, and "sweat equity" from the CEO to the lowest-ranking employee in pursuit of the goals of the plan.

Proactive planning helps the institution reach a higher level of distinction by producing and carrying out a plan that elevates the college and the community to a new level of purpose—one that seemed beyond the collective grasp of either before the process began.

Proactive planning changes the institutional climate so that a greater number of employees, in all categories, develop a level of reasoned dissatisfaction with the status quo and a willingness to invest time and energy, despite perceived risks, to help move the institution forward.

Proactive planning is value-based in order to bring about results that are meaningful and cause vexing issues to reach a level of organizational credibility that was not present when planning started. Value-based planning allows guiding beliefs and strong preferences, which are usually divergent, to be forged into a collective value system that pins the planning process and the plan together.

Proactive planning is adaptive so that a planning congruity exists between the organization and its external environment. Proactive planning requires an institution to adapt its role to meet the needs of the community rather than the self-interest of the institution or its planners. Being adaptive also demands that institutions clearly define their capabilities—what they can reasonably do and not do.

Adaptive planning causes institutions to adjust planning requirements to meet the needs of school drop-outs, women in transition, illiterates, the unemployed, and others whose conditions hamper our systems, overburden our budgets, and waste human potential.

To the extent that planning has these eleven characteristics, our chances of making good on the opportunities of a new decade and a new century will be actualized. Our generation of community college planners—the fourth—has the greatest challenge and the greatest potential for success!

In the earlier periods that marked the development of the nation's community, junior, and technical colleges, there was an almost missionary zeal toward facing challenges and creatively solving them. In the decade ahead, our institutions must somehow capture anew that same zeal if we are to respond effectively to the many complex issues that face our world, our nation, and our communities.

It has been suggested that community colleges are the eagle's nest of higher education. Like the eagle, our colleges must demonstrate the strength, size, gracefulness, keenness of vision, and propensity for action that is required of an eagle guarding its nest.

Characteristics of the eagle will not come easily. The challenge will require an institutional self-discipline that is difficult to achieve in a society as confused and musing as ours. It will test our willpower, our mettle, and our resolve. Such characteristics will not be imposed solely from external sources. America's community colleges must both desire and aspire to significantly impact the needs, issues, and opportunities of our time. Then, and only then, will our 1,211 institutions truly soar.

Dan Angel is president and Mike DeVault is executive assistant to the president at Austin Community College, Austin, Texas.

CHAPTER TWO

Environmental Scanning

By James L. Catanzaro

A S I LOOK back over twenty-five years of professional service, two experiences intersect relating to the importance of environmental scanning. The first experience was with an emerging California community college in the mid-'60s. The second was an executive stint in the mid-'70s in a large corporation that was aggressively engaged in growth by acquisitions and new ventures.

The community college experience was the most gratifying of my career. A new college was being planned in the district where I was teaching, and I had the good fortune of being asked to be part of the initial administrative team. We spent the summer planning the programs of the new college, designing the curricula, and master planning the campus. We thought we did these things with a high level of expertise. I suppose, given the kinds of people we had on the team and the consultants we brought in, we did quite well within our time constraints.

A decade later, I left education for an executive assignment in a corporation. The firm was facing similar challenges. It was fast building new activities, some from the ground up. We were scouting out companies across the country for purchase, and we were launching new operations.

Today, I am struck by the differences in approach. In fact, the two processes were like night and day. At the community college we spent essentially a summer in informal meetings thinking out what our college could and would be. We did this with very little research. In the corporation, formal, highly disciplined preparations went into each new venture and acquisition. Each was research-based, and each element in the process was identified and carefully considered.

In the college setting we came up with some ideas and a plan for flexible physical structures and a striking campus. We had a good base: a parent college. So we took the things that we liked from the parent and discarded those things we didn't like, and we looked around the state of California for other ideas. (We thought anything east of the California border was primitive by comparison, so we spent little time reflecting on what was done elsewhere!)

In any case, we brought together some exciting concepts, and the school started with a tremendous amount of enthusiasm. Three to four years later, however, the enthusiasm had waned. There was a period of struggle to get back the momentum, but time showed that the foundation was not so firm. We had made some fundamental errors of judgment.

In the corporate setting our expansion occurred quite differently. Through many hours of team meetings we developed a detailed portfolio of the resources available for expansion; we crystallized our purpose; and we specifically operationalized how we could achieve our goals. Most important, we had an overriding concern that limited resources be spent optimally. Therefore, we matched resources to the process of mission accomplishment. Without calling it strategic planning (because it wasn't a term we knew), we did just that. We were alert to threats and opportunities, and we were aware of precisely how our resources could be developed to avert the threats and maximize opportunities.

How can these two experiences be examined in order to provide helpful advice to institutions engaged in planning?

In the community college venture our best ideas were put together in order to describe the path that we would take. We tried to think of what our college would look like three, five, seven years down the road. But we didn't have an understanding of the college once it was operating, especially given its very distinctive environment and specific resources. Most important, we did not consider how our new efforts would impact upon the traditional activities of the college.

We had some unique ideas, but if you go back to our early mission statement, you can see that what we authored could have been taken to any number of community colleges and added to their literature and no one would have noticed a difference. In fact, we could have saved ourselves a lot of time by borrowing more of the work of others.

We projected a new and different college, but what was new was not environmentally shaped. We didn't pay enough attention to environmental features in order to distinctively shape the college's activity and life. Further, we failed to reflect sufficiently on the character of the new organization we were building and the possibilities within that organization. We certainly didn't recognize that we had to self-consciously position ourselves in order to maximize opportunities and to make full use of our resources—human, financial, physical, environmental, even emotive. We did not operate in these terms. As a result, we fell short of our true potential.

Worse, we launched the school into directions that people to this day say we should never have considered. We put enormous resources into the Postlewaite audio tutorial system. We were convinced it was the wave of the future. It wasn't, and the specialized labs were pulled out in a few years.

We also put extraordinary resources into television instruction. As the years have demonstrated, more than 95 percent of the regular faculty did not become involved in television because they had little interest in it, didn't have the aptitude for it, or wouldn't put in the time. They were good at teaching in a traditional setting, but they weren't particularly adept at working with television as a medium of instruction. Subsequently, television production turned out to be a poor investment.

Equally significant, we didn't know television ourselves. The preparatory work that has to go into a course was only dimly recognized. We didn't realize that there aren't many faculty out there who want to give up every other obligation to do television, and we did not know the requirements of producing a television course on a professional level.

These kinds of misjudgments can be avoided.

In the corporation, emerging activities ran much truer to prediction even though the firm's marketplace was much more volatile. Resources were deployed effectively, and the results were measurably better. The reason is obvious: our preparation was more thorough.

With these two different experiences in mind, my first admonition in planning is this: Begin with an analysis of your specific environment and plan accordingly so you can be positioned as an organization to take maximum advantage of the opportunities that are presented. Start from where you are and who you are.

Recently I was in the office of the CEO of M&M Mars, a Chicagoland company. I asked the CEO, "Why are you here? Isn't Chicago an expensive place for a candy maker to be?" His answer: "Wisconsin is nearby; that's dairy farm country. Candy bars are basically made of milk products. Chicago is the center of national distribution because of location and rail and air systems. Therefore, Chicago is the right place for candy making. That's why we're here. We wouldn't be any other place." Makes good sense! M&M Mars was positioned 75 years ago to be where it could take maximum advantage of the opportunity of making candy bars cheaply and distributing them across the country from a central point.

We have to begin by thinking in terms of what our unique position is and can be, so we can take advantage of the range of possibilities available to us. Each college has a unique environment and therefore unique possibilities.

Of course, with a specific setting comes a specific set of threats. Admonition number two is this: Describe the competitive elements in your environment. No college sits in isolation. Most have other colleges around them. Many have proprietary schools, universities, even corporate training activities that compete for students. There are always some competitors out there, some constraints to development. Take them fully into account.

Competitors suggest we haven't reached (and, to some degree, can't reach) our full potential. Most of us have a long way to go to optimize opportunities. It takes planning to extend our reach and effectiveness, planning based on knowledge of the threats to our success.

Effective planning is, then, planning out a future that will help maximize potential and take effective control of what is controllable so that outside forces as well as internal forces won't defeat our efforts. That's what makes it different from traditional planning efforts that are not based on environmental scanning for opportunities and threats.

Internal forces are also important to recognize in our plans. In developing a new college, we didn't envision that three or four years down the road the excitement would be gone, interdepartmental struggles would emerge, and such events would sap our energy. We did not recognize that our will to move forward with the verve and intensity of the past could be weakened. Internal dynamics, including attitudes toward success, are critical elements of an effective plan.

If the owner of a professional sports team says, "I think we will end up in the middle of the pack this year," you can be sure the team will come in last. To be able to end up respectably you have to shoot for number one. So it is with community colleges. We must have vision to be in a position to take control of our future and to achieve at a distinguished level. Otherwise, internal drains on energy and external constraints will defeat us. Admonition three is, therefore: Have lofty aspirations.

Given these three general admonitions, successful planning begins by conducting a trend analysis of virtually every college activity and every characteristic of your district. Look back five to seven years in order to project three to five years forward. Try to capture the trends. Take your measurements in continuum form, in other words. Look for the patterns—even in attitudes. What did people think of our possibilities five years ago? What do they think of them now? The answers to such questions must then be assembled and presented in trend form.

Once the trends are known, then the larger environment, both internal and external, will be revealed. At that point we should inquire, "What are those things that present themselves to us now that are distinct opportunities we can seize upon given capability and will? What are those things that can work against negative trends and reinforce positive trends?" It is likely that people in the school know these right now. There are faculty members, staff, and administrators who know the "helps" and the "hinders." They must now be called upon to add these to the information base. A college must understand what those obstacles are so it can isolate and control them as well.

This activity, in sum, consists of consulting your colleagues in order to identify the "helps" to growth. These should be listed and then prioritized. Decide which are closest to your central mission, to the basic values of your institution, and which are urgent to your organization's future success. Decide which are manageable—which you can do without blocking other things you want to do. Assess which things are going to cost you in personnel time, which are going to have an impact on other challenges and opportunities. Reflect on how people in the external environment will perceive them. After all, the political impact of decision making must be taken into account also.

Once there is a general consensus on the priority order, it is likely that agreement on direction will emerge. At that point, enlist the most talented people in the organization to set forth an action plan, which should include goals and how they can be achieved, time frames, and resource determinations.

The plan, however, has to be operationalized to be of value. This takes concerted effort. Thus, the final step that often separates corporate behavior from typical college behavior is this: conjoint execution.

Goal achievement is a hard thing to do in education because of our reliance on formal organizational structures. In the corporation when we had goals that we urgently needed to achieve, the president would assign responsibility to the appropriate vice president, but along with that assignment he would form action teams of those he felt had the brain power, the execution skills, the background, the time, the energy, the vision to get the job done. The president used to comment: "We're just going to take them out of their departments and drop them in here, part-time, full-time, an hour, a day, whatever is necessary. We are going to get this job done!"

We threw our best talent at our best challenges in a single-minded fashion, and we moved beyond the formal organizational structure to do so. In so doing, we were resourceful. This is a tremendously powerful approach. It involves the "risk" of having people at different levels of the organization involved in high-level work, and the "risk" of taking people from one area and involving them in another. Above all, it means pooled ingenuity.

The behavior that is seen in colleges far more than in the corporate community is general participation in the total strategic planning process—done usually to achieve a wide sense of ownership. But this practice often leads to planning failure, because if the plan is developed by everyone, then there will be no truly unifying plan, just a document most any college could adopt. Value may be realized through the process, but the plan itself will be insufficient. It is systematically better to have a representative group of incisive thinkers forge a draft document that can be reviewed by the total college community, than it is to include many at the start and produce an attenuated document.

Finally, what is produced must be seen always as preliminary pathfinding. Planning is a continuing effort. It is an ongoing commitment to determine how a particular college can be positioned so that years ahead the school is consummately using its limited resources for the best interests of students and the district. It is a continuous effort to marshal resources to achieve excellence.

The process is also ongoing because the challenge is ongoing. As the effort moves forward, it gives new life and new enthusiasm to the institution and its members. Mix that enthusiasm with a carefully crafted portfolio of available resources, a clear understanding of the college's mission in conjunction with area needs, and operational plans of how to achieve that mission in the face of known constraints, and the possibilities are virtually limitless.

You must have lofty aspirations to succeed, but you must have research-based plans to engineer achievement.

James L. Catanzaro is president of Chattanooga State Technical Community College in Chattanooga, Tennessee.

CHAPTER THREE

Management and Change Through the Planning Process

By Richard McDowell

AMERICAN COMMUNITY COLLEGES have undergone significant changes over the past twenty-five years and will continue to change in complexity and purpose in the next decade. Planning for the future opportunities that these changes will bring creates anticipation and excitement. Planning involves not only predicting the future, but also creating it. Pride in our colleges motivates us to do that planning.

An important element of planning is goal setting. The comic strip "Shoe" by Jeff McNelly helps us examine goal setting. Shoe is sitting at his typewriter listing his goals. His short-term goal is to make it to 5 p.m. His long-term goal is to string together a whole bunch of short-term goals!

Reprinted by permission: Tribune Media Services.

In our jobs we often don't take the time to think beyond getting through the rest of the week, the semester, or the academic year. Planning helps us develop a long-range view of the future of the college.

Planning involves deciding to change. No decision is a decision not to change. One of my favorite poems about change is "The Calf Path." The poem indicates that over 200 years ago, a calf meandered through the woods on its way home. In subsequent years, people, and later horses and wagons, followed along that path. Eventually, this crooked path became a road, which was paved and widened and became the center of a town. People who followed that road probably wondered why it was so crooked, but they didn't do anything about straightening it out.

The poem communicates that many times we continue to do things the same way over and over because that's the way we've always done it.

The planning process provides the opportunity to evaluate our colleges' operations and come up with some ideas on how they can be improved. It's not legitimate to continue to do the same thing over and over, because the college will not improve but instead will end up like that crooked path that becomes a grand but crooked boulevard.

Some people may not be interested in planning for change because it's too much work (One of our faculty members says every time he finally gets organized, he gets a new dean who makes him change things all around and he has to start all over again). Others are most comfortable with routine. Many people are unwilling to participate in planning for change because their past recommendations were not implemented.

However, there are circumstances under which change is acceptable. For example, George Steiner tells us that change is more acceptable when it's understood than when it's not, and it's more acceptable when it does not threaten security than when it does. He indicates that it's more acceptable when those affected have helped to create it, rather than when it's been externally imposed. We have all had the experience of receiving a memo that says that "effective immediately" a change will take place in some college procedure. It may affect parking, distribution of paychecks, or other sensitive issues. The memo does not provide the staff an opportunity to respond. The memo usually causes a negative reaction, resulting in meetings to discuss alternative solutions, which should have occurred in the first place. We've done away with "effective immediately" memos at our college.

Change is more acceptable if it's been planned than if it's experimental, and it is more acceptable to people new on the job than to people old on the job (Steiner). However, willingness to change is probably more attributable to personality than to age. Change is also more acceptable to people who benefit from the change (Steiner).

Elements of Good Planning

What are some of the key steps in developing a good plan for a community college? One is creating and communicating a shared vision, the dreams and hopes of the staff and board of the college about what the college can become. Presidential leadership is important in transforming those dreams into a strong commitment and dedication by the staff to make them a reality. The president also has the responsibility to constantly remind people what that vision is and how well the college is doing in fulfilling that vision.

The second element of good planning is to establish values. Values indicate the basic beliefs of the college staff and board and what makes your college unique and different from other colleges. What characteristics describe the uniqueness of your college? Is your college one that stresses learning and excellence in the classroom? Does it have a caring environment for students and staff? Is your college one that relates to the needs of the community? Would you like your college to be known as one that stresses innovation? Is one of your values your staff's responsiveness to requests for services? Is one having the highest student retention or success rate? Your planning process should include some discussion, clarification, and statement of the values of your college.

The third element of successful planning is to develop a participatory planning process. People who participate in the planning process develop ownership of the plan and will work hard to see that it is accomplished.

How do we get maximum participation in our planning efforts? A successful strategy is to take people who are willing to investigate change and work through them. Some people will wait to see if you are going to be successful before they participate. The more you accomplish, the more they will want to be involved, because they will believe you are serious. Some people like the routine they have and will keep doing things the same way forever. You can encourage people to participate, but if they don't, your responsibility is to move ahead anyway and not wait until you have 100 percent participation.

A fourth element is to be action-oriented. You must respond in a timely manner to suggestions from the staff and students. A response indicates that they and their opinions are important. Lack of response frustrates them. Of particular importance are requests for building repairs because they are very visible. It is also important to keep our buildings clean and in good repair because it communicates quality and caring. Likewise, dirty halls, restrooms, and cafeterias create a negative image. A campus where the grass is cut and flowers are blooming creates a sense of pride in the staff and students.

The fifth element is care and feeding of staff. You must establish good relationships with the staff and help them grow.

The Schoolcraft Experience

When I came to Schoolcraft College, a college of 9,200 students in Livonia, Michigan, I decided to develop a five-year plan using the five elements of successful planning. Calling on all departments of the college for input, our resulting plan has improved college service in a number of areas and strengthened the institution internally in the process. I offer our experience as a road map to successful planning for medium-sized colleges.

One of our strategies was to examine those things that were impeding good staff relations and deal with them. Our major problem was collective bargaining; in the 1970s, the faculty at our college conducted three labor strikes. When I arrived we decided to investigate a cooperative collective bargaining process. We tried it and it has worked well. The old process involved power plays and "winners" and "losers." It was very frustrating, and neither side felt satisfied when a contract was negotiated. In the new process, everyone is a winner, and improvements are implemented that make the college better. It also strengthens the relationship between the administration and the staff.

We have begun a number of staff development and recognition programs. We have developed retraining programs, sent people to conferences, and brought speakers on campus. We have developed an employee assistance program to help people with problems related to drugs, alcohol, relationships among family members, and employee wellness. We started a program to recognize our staff for years of service and outstanding contributions to the college. We have developed "quality of work life" programs where employee groups meet and make suggestions about their work situations.

We have initiated orientation programs for new employees. We found that a great time to meet and talk with a person who is going to be an important member of the staff is when that person is hired as a new employee. We help them get acquainted and develop the right attitude about working in a particular department. New employees are taken on a tour of the college, and somebody from their department takes them to lunch. We also have videotapes that provide information about the college and introduce them to the staff.

One of the best techniques for positive staff relations is face-to-face communications. We spend considerable time walking around campus and talking with the staff. On one of my walks, one of the faculty members said, "Things seem to be going pretty well here." Now, being a typical administrator, I was anxious to take credit for those good things. So, I said, "Oh, yes. That's because of all the new staff programs we started." She said, "No, it's because you come around and talk to us. You know who we are by name, you listen to us, and you care about what we're doing." She was right. Knowing who your employees are and caring about what they do is a powerful motivator.

We begin our planning process with a review of our mission statement. Goals are developed, and each unit within the college comes up with objectives that state how they are going to help the college achieve those goals, as well as other activities in which that department is going to be involved.

Each department develops a five-year plan, and that plan becomes the basis for our budgeting. As the plans are submitted, we review them and indicate when certain items, such as purchasing a piece of equipment or hiring a new staff member, will be done. If we don't agree on an item, we continue discussing it. If a department has not submitted a plan, it doesn't get any increased funds (It is amazing how that encourages staff to submit a plan). We now have a five-year plan for each department.

Eight college planning goals were developed, but I will note only two of them. One goal was to provide for the financial stability of the college. To accomplish this goal, we examined current revenue sources and developed new ones. We continued to lobby the legislature for more state aid. We held a millage election to increase our local taxes and examined the tuition rate set by the board of trustees.

We also revitalized the college foundation and, as a result, we've raised over $850,000. We use the money to create an endowment that funds scholarships and the purchase of instructional equipment.

Another project that produces significant revenue is our land development project. We are fortunate because the college is located near an expressway where there is a lot of commercial development. We had the opportunity to lease some of our college land to a developer on a long-term lease. The developer has built office buildings and a restaurant on the land, and will manage the buildings, rent the offices, and return a significant amount of money to the college. We will use the money to build a new building and to make permanent improvements. This money will provide for the long-term financial needs of the college.

Another goal was to provide for the quality of instructional programs. All of our programs were evaluated to determine to what degree they were meeting students' needs. The programs were evaluated by the instructors, administrators, students, advisory committee members, employers, and representatives from institutions to which our students transfer. We updated the programs, retrained instructors, purchased equipment, and replaced the tablet armchairs in the classrooms with tables and chairs so the adult students could be more comfortable. We have also taken a look at the way we hire faculty. We not only review their credentials, but we also may ask them to teach a class or present a videotape of them teaching before we hire them.

We have also developed some "General Education Goals" that identify what a student should learn as a result of attending our college and earning an associate degree. These requirements identify skill levels and knowledge a student will attain in math, writing, speaking and listening, reasoning, computer technology, and science.

We have gone even further and developed the "Assurance of Quality Statement," which guarantees our students' competencies to employers or institutions to which our students transfer. If a student does not have the competency he or she should have learned in a particular class, the student can return and re-enroll in the class at no cost. We think it is important to be able to certify the competencies of our students.

The management of change through the planning process has resulted in an improvement in the operation of Schoolcraft and has established the college's future direction.

Richard McDowell is president of Schoolcraft College in Livonia, Michigan.

CHAPTER FOUR

Institutional Renewal

By Paul Elsner

THREE FORCES HAVE shaped my thinking about community colleges. The first happened three years ago when I got involved with the faculty from the Theater Arts and English departments and wrote a twenty-first century morality play based on what I thought the community college movement might be facing five or ten years down the road. The play presented challenges of the past, present, and future.

The second major event happened when I served on the AACJC Commission on the Future of Community Colleges. I was pleased that the theme "Building Communities" emerged from the commission's work.

The third area of ideological formation for me was my involvement with Campus Compact. This is a national program involving the promotion of social responsibility among young people, but it could have been addressed to a lot of other groups.

My sense is that we are now going through a philosophical and ideological struggle with what the community college movement really is about. We have been a part of higher education and we have been a part of the secondary schools. We have emerged as sort of a segment between the two, but we are neither fish nor fowl; we are somewhere in-between.

We are in search of a new methodology. We must learn to work with wide ranges of people who require family support, literacy training, adult education, and other kinds of services. In a fashion, we are brokering other social service agencies to try to bring forth some kind of reconstruction of the neighborhoods around which our community colleges are building. This community building or bonding is not an agenda that we are necessarily ready to tackle.

Despite these looming social problems that exist around us, we may be the only institutions in a position to respond—whether we are ready or not. The community colleges that will dominate the next decade will be the institutions who learn this new methodology.

This does not mean that we compromise our standards as collegiate institutions, but rather that we strengthen the pipeline of students who are coming to us. We must forge the kind of future institution that will meet their needs. Greater numbers than ever before are not at all prepared for collegiate-level work.

My home city of Phoenix is by all perceptions an affluent Sun Belt community, yet in the feeder high schools in the Phoenix Union High School District, more Hispanic youth age fifteen and older drop out than in El Paso,

Las Cruces, Albuquerque, and San Antonio, both percentage-wise and numerically. More people aged fifteen to eighteen are on the streets and not in school in Phoenix than in any other city in the Southwest.

We had 1,481 pregnancies—three a day—in the Phoenix Union High School District last year. Many of these babies weighed less than five pounds. We are not talking about the casual disintegration of the social neighborhood and community fabric. We are talking about a deep and serious crisis.

Part of our responsibility as community college educators is to know what the conditions are in our local communities. Do the public school systems that feed students into our system have a significant drop-out problem? Our institutions should be a catalyst for change by reducing the number of drop-outs and working with young single parents for whom there is little hope. To some degree one city is simply a microcosm for our nation. How one of our institutions responds should help each of us to respond. This isn't the time to duck and hide!

We are moving more and more toward a two-tiered society. In one portion of this society, we are all basically entitled people with some degree of affluence. The second tier does not participate at all, does not have a way to even put its act together. These are the single parents who come into our classes, who say they have been kicked out of their apartments because they cannot pay their rent. These are the students who cannot get their cars running in the morning, who cannot afford taxi fare. These are real, everyday problems for a normal community college student.

We need to think more expansively about urban dormitories in urban areas. Housing is one of the most serious problems students face. We do not want to accept that, but there are all kinds of signals given to young people to leave home. Many high school students do not live at home at the time they graduate. They may have experienced stress at home, step-parent arrangements, divorce, or some other breakdown of the family, and they live elsewhere, usually at economic peril to themselves.

Think for a moment what it takes to go to school and live in a home or an apartment. The average cost of the lowest studio one-bedroom apartment in the Los Angeles basin is now $475 a month. It does not take very long to realize what kind of income you have to make to keep up $475-a-month payments. Many cannot do it.

The building of communities requires us to learn how to integrate, broker, match, and reconstitute our institutions as well as form new institutions from institutions that are already working. Many times we think of ourselves as a community college, but we may have to think of community development centers, skill centers, and other kinds of arrangements as we evolve as an institution. There may have to be many of them, in multiple locations.

The historical evolution of Campus Compact, the third great influence on me, probably came from the UCLA studies in attitudes of incoming freshmen.

Freshmen used to cite finding a meaningful philosophy of life as very important. Finding a job and making money has replaced this goal in recent years. The studies said that 80 percent want to make money. We say that is too high. Actually, 40 percent wanted to make money. The other 40 percent wanted to make a hell of a lot of money!

How do you instill attitudes toward social responsibility among these students? This is not an easy task. Father Timothy Healy, former president of Georgetown University, argues that it is going to be tough to instill social responsibility because the notion of the university usually precludes it. In the minds of many, the purpose of the university is to develop the intellect, not necessarily the whole person. That is true of the university in general. Teaching well is not always rewarded. So you are really bucking the tide when you discuss civic and social responsibility around some colleges and universities.

Students are anxious to participate in socially responsible activities if they are given the opportunity to participate in the structure or design of these activities. Moreover, they are even more committed if they are able to be part of recruiting other students to that activity.

We have over 3,200 students working in volunteer activities at Maricopa County Community Colleges. This is a new extension of the volunteerism philosophy of student services. Is student volunteerism a priority on your campus? The student services offices across the network of community colleges should be in the vanguard of promoting socially conscious and socially active students. There are many community problems that our students could address if they were invigorated with commitment and energy. It is our responsibility to invigorate them!

There are dangers as well as benefits to integrating community service groups with education. Congress has a bill that would tie community service to financial aid. Bad deal. What you want to do is have that as an option for students, not a substitute. The poor will end up doing community service for their financial aid, and the wealthy will just pay for college. We do not want to get in that trap. Nonetheless, volunteerism is powerful. If we could figure out how to integrate volunteerism with the educational program, it would be wonderful. The idea of loan forgiveness for doing community work seems to be a good one.

The faculty association president at my college says, "I don't think we can get everybody to do volunteerism, but I bet we can get all the new ones to commit three hours to community service as part of their philosophy of working for our district." Will they be willing to do it? Maybe. Sometimes the failure is ours. Sometimes we do not ask people to do things. Sometimes we do not ask them in the right way. Leadership requires that we ask important questions and establish priorities that require our institutions to be more responsible for building better communities.

I do not know where we will be by the middle of the next decade, but I think we will establish some kind of service premise at Maricopa that will be different from some of the other institutions around the country. It is important that every institution establish a service philosophy that extends beyond the bricks and mortar of campus buildings.

In Rochester, New York, the school district made dramatic changes in how it conducts business. First, the school district negotiated a contract with teachers that raised beginning salaries to $29,000 a year and top salaries to $70,000. Dramatic as those figures are, they are only part of the story, and perhaps not the most interesting part.

The Rochester district also introduced a career ladder that will allow teachers to become master teachers by moving through various stages and meeting various criteria. Master teachers will be asked to use their energy and talent in the schools that now have the highest turnover and serve the least advantaged students. Some of the inner-city schools staffed by master teachers will also be schools for the professional development of incoming teachers. The dual goal is to produce highly qualified teachers for schools throughout the system and offer state-of-the-art education to children who have traditionally been the least well-served.

How are we to staff these enormously powerful institutions with master teachers in the next decade, particularly as more poorly prepared students arrive at our door?

The director of the National Science Foundation announced last year that 50 percent of all graduate students in pacesetting, research-based universities and colleges were foreign nationals. Community colleges do not have a pipeline of strong science faculty coming up through the system. Board members must think about how they are going to position their institutions to get the most qualified teachers in the country for the most important segment of delivery for the nation. Are we up to this challenge?

Think about the flow of minority applicants for teaching positions and how you are going to have to intervene at your colleges to make the pipeline effective. Throughout the United States, we only graduated a half-dozen minority Ph.D.s in computer science in the last year.

What are the major issues we must think about in the '90s?

• We have to deal with an increasingly two-tiered society where one group in the society is relatively well-off and the other group is barely surviving and may even be permanently disenfranchised. Some have referred to the latter group as the permanent underclass.

• We have to come up with a whole different model for linking schools and working with younger students in the grade schools and in the high schools—a formalized institutional think tank is a good model.

• We have to strengthen the core functions of our institutions. We have healthy outreach programs, such as industry programs for returning working adults, but we have lost some of our critical mass. Too few of our students take a block of studies. We are becoming an institution of 100 agendas and one-course students. We have to maintain, in our community colleges, the strength of the common core of general education requirements and keep those programs strong. I am worried that 37 percent of the 86,000 students at Maricopa County Community Colleges take only one class. We cannot get people to think about a block of study or continuity in their educational program when so many are taking only a course or two. This high percentage is typical of colleges around the nation.

We must boldly move into the international agenda and address world competitiveness as a central agenda of our time.

Issues of amnesty and immigration have to be addressed and wrestled with. Miami-Dade Community College and Los Angeles City College enroll the largest numbers of F–1 students in all of higher education. We must acknowledge this diversity in our strategic plans.

Finally, we have to think of the future cadre of leaders and faculty for our institutions.

If we do not think about the above problems, we risk disaster. As institutions that have historically found great pride in responding to local needs, our colleges will continue to lose ground if we don't acknowledge what is going on around us.

A new social entrepreneurship is emerging in our colleges, a new social reconstruction that community colleges should be and have to be a part of. We have the expertise in our faculty and staff. We have the will to become involved in meaningful ways. The most distinguished community colleges in the country, those that are doing what they need to be doing, have these kinds of social agendas in place. Community building and reconstruction are the agenda of the future. They are the agenda for our youth. They form the agenda for the twenty-first century.

Paul Elsner is the chancellor of Maricopa County Community College District in Phoenix, Arizona.

CHAPTER FIVE

Vision and Vitality

By Carl Kuttler

THE FOREMOST ELEMENT in leadership is vision. To be effective, we must keep our eyes on the horizon. As Satchel Paige said, "Don't look back; they may be gainin' on you." The horizon today shimmers with change. Let's take a look at it and see some of the key factors in planning.

• The graying of America. Eighty percent of the work force in 2001 is already out of high school. We must provide for an older population seeking new career skills and interesting avocations.

• The coloring of America. This nation has a minority population rising to equal one-third of the populace. If our colleges are to continue to be the door of access to opportunity—and we must be that door—we must serve minorities in new and better ways to avoid the creation of what Franklin Roosevelt worried would be a permanent underclass.

• The internationalization of our economy. Not one of the world's ten largest banks is in America. Forty percent of the parts used in American manufacturing were made outside the United States last year. We must aid business and industry as it retools and retrains.

Community colleges are perfectly poised to become the catalysts for a competitive America. We are in touch with the world of commerce. We know our nearby businesses. We know our communities. We need only to extend our hands to form partnerships that will make a difference in the work force and the marketplace.

Let me offer a 95-cent word here that defines what I mean by partnerships. The word is synergism, and here's how Webster defines it:

The cooperative action of discrete agencies such that the total effect is greater than the sum of the effects taken independently.

It's what happens when a private foundation enables a college to work with a business to create new learning outcomes that will benefit society. Or, when an insurance company gave a building with over 130,000 square feet and 20 acres of land to St. Petersburg Junior College, which sought to make it a drug law enforcement education center at a time when the nation groaned with the perils of drug abuse. The days are over when a good budget could be built entirely on tax revenue. Private sector support must be developed and maintained.

The horizon also rumbles with the tremors of new technology. Fifteen years ago, the United States was the unassailable leader in the semiconductor industry. No more. Computerization of our world does not just mean the accumulation of data. Computerized decisions will be next. The key word for coping with technology is flexibility, and community colleges have that characteristic.

Knowledge itself is expanding. Today the half-life of an engineer's knowledge is down to five years. Yet, as knowledge expands and as we learn more about things, will we continue to learn about humanity, about interpersonal relations, about values? Will the only way we value our college be in headcounts and dollars? We can no longer assume that the institutions of family, church, synagogue, or service organization will inculcate those key values that make America good.

The historian Alexis de Tocqueville worried that when America ceased to be good, it would cease to be great. College leaders must keep an eye on the horizon. They must keep an eye on the human dimension, on the heart. College budgets need to reflect compassion internally as well as competition internationally.

By our attitude and support, we can unleash the genius and creativity of our faculty and staff; indeed, we can empower our institutions. By our spirit and style, we can promote openness and accessibility. We can foster an atmosphere where college leaders can dare to take risks, to create an invention or an innovation, to develop a new idea for the nation—not just a better mousetrap, but a better community. If we do not engender this kind of leadership and initiative, who will?

Former President Jimmy Carter, speaking to community college presidents at a national forum on the role of community colleges in shaping the nation, said

> I think that the responsibility, the initiative ought to be yours, to go to the employers and say, "What can we do to improve the quality of our present graduates, and what can we do to provide the potential employees that you will need in the future?" Unless you (the community college) take the initiative, I don't see any other place for it to be taken. Who else in your community would see the disparity between graduates and job opportunities? Who else besides you could judge the difference between the education students get and their performance on the job?

If that's not creative planning, what is?

Our job, then, is to encourage all of our colleagues to focus on giving America that competitive edge.

The pursuit of excellence in the president's office and in the college begins with our commitment to excellence in the people we hire and lead. The achievements we may expect from others begin with our own effort at vision and vitality.

What happens to one community college can be achieved in many others. Each institution should attempt to read the signals and currents and ask the question, "How can my institution respond?" At St. Petersburg Junior College (SPJC), each time we responded to one signal, opportunities opened up in many other ways. That is what can and should happen in each community, junior, and technical college across the country.

When I was speaking to a meeting of Texas trustees in Austin three years ago, sharing our academic program over breakfast, three national leaders challenged me to what later became a roundtable. St. Petersburg Junior College invited the professorial types who have college leadership doctoral programs in the United States—the Pat Crosses, the John Roueches, the Lou Benders, and the Jim Wattenbargers—to take a look and to tell us where our holes were. It was painful.

The first question out of the roundtable that I was asked, and I flunked it, was this: What is the difference between administration and leadership? You can be an administrator and administer well, but you can still be doing the wrong thing. It's like doing a good job building Hula-Hoops when there's no market. You can administer the right thing poorly, you can administer poorly the wrong thing, or you can administer, correctly, the right thing. Leadership is doing the right thing, and administration is doing the right thing well. And you need both.

During a second roundtable, some of the Washington, D.C., education leadership were invited to take a look at SPJC, including representatives of the American Council on Education, the American Vocational Association, and the Harvard School of Education. Eighteen came. They gave us more ideas. Very little was being done in international education at the time. We also learned new ideas from several Latin American presidents at a Carter Center program. One of the things that was learned was that every year the Soviet Union fully supports 90,000 students from around the world and gives them free scholarships. Thirteen thousand are from Latin America, 900 are from Panama. When the Kissinger Commission did its landmark study of Latin America, do you know what they found? Not one student from Panama was in America.

Do you know what they're studying in the Soviet Union? Waterway management. Do you get the idea of what's going to take place in Panama with 900 students studying waterway management in the Soviet Union? It's already beginning to happen.

You should brainstorm about how to lend a hand in these efforts. Right now, former Presidents Carter and Ford are asking governors for a scholarship program that allows every community college in America to admit ten students from Latin America free. That will be 12,240 students, and we will equal what the Soviet Union is doing, and at a low cost. Can a community college make a difference? I think each one can. Can the movement? You better believe it. You potentially can change Latin and South America.

After another roundtable, this time at the Gerald Ford Library in Grand Rapids, Michigan, and the subsequent publication of St. *Petersburg Junior College—On the Cutting Edge*, SPJC began talking with a large company. Soon, an $11-million gift had been presented to our institution. Another Fortune 500 company read about that, picked up the phone, and asked if they could talk to us. And then the insurance company that gave us the building came back and said, "We're fighting drugs in America. Would you accept $30,000 to do something for fighting drugs?" In January 1990 we staged a national symposium, "Drug Law Enforcement in the Year 2000." We involved the International Police Association, the drug enforcement people, the FBI training people, the National Institute of Justice, and many others.

We recently had a developing situation in Florida on mandatory assessment. We learned of proposed legislation that would mandate a 12,000-word writing requirement in English. Administration just says, you're going to do what you've been told. Leadership asks: What was the legislature trying to say? What is the legislature saying to each school and how well are we answering them with results? Legislators mandated standards because we hadn't done enough. Communication was mandated because there was a perception that we weren't communicating. We brainstormed and realized that if they were asking us to have writing courses, they were really talking about communication. Therefore, SPJC decided, in addition to the English writing requirements, to add a 2,000-word writing requirement in fifty other courses and to make speech courses mandatory, because students should be able to speak as well as write.

Out of that came assessment tests. Though often bemoaned, these tests can pose an opportunity for institutional growth. Realizing that tests at the graduation level would soon be mandatory for community college students, and wanting to look good on those tests, SPJC gave its own test to students. When some students demonstrated that they were not ready to take the state test, we established review courses and a course called "College Survival Skills," which, perhaps, should be considered by every community college in America.

Former U.S. Education Secretary Terrel Bell signed a contract recently with our institution to chair a commission on putting together a distinctive academic plan for teachers in the year 2000. Nurses in Florida have fourteen continuing education hours, lawyers have a certain number of hours, doctors have them, and educators, who teach so much training, have few if any. And if you look at most certification requirements, they're miserable, including ours. But we want to do better.

What about the student center? We learned that the legislature felt that there was too much playing going on. We got rid of some of our pool tables and put in personal computers—PCs in the student lounge in a designated area so students could practice instead of wasting time. We're negotiating with a computer company that's looking at giving every faculty member a computer.

When we shared this idea with a foundation, its officers said, "Can we possibly be involved and give you money for the staff development for your faculty?" Earl Nightingale has written:

> Successful people are dreamers who have found a dream too exciting and too important to remain in the realm of fantasy, and who, day by day and hour by hour, toil in the service of their dream until they can touch it with their hands and see it with their eyes.

The community, technical, and junior colleges are part of a uniquely American dream. We are the lone American innovation among the education institution models of the world. We are now one of America's proudest exports.

Community colleges have become the eagle's nest of American education. Under their wings, one of every two high school graduates begins the college experience. Under their wings, two of every three minority students find access to higher education. And under their wings, businesses find their partnerships for education and retraining to help make America competitive in the international marketplace.

As we approach the year 2000, our role will be to help build nests nurturing our students. Yes, we may have to push a little to help some of the eagles get airborne, but we must face that responsibility if more and more Americans are to enjoy the opportunity to pursue their dreams.

Carl Kuttler is president of St. Petersburg Junior College in St. Petersburg, Florida.

CHAPTER SIX

Value-Based Actions

By Peter M. Hirsch

E VERY SINGLE DECISION we make, every single one, has its basis in values, whether those values are moral, ethical, economic, or personal. There's absolutely no way to hide from that; we must recognize this fact and meet it head on.

I am not the first person to make this observation. Max Weber, in his writings, made a career of arguing with Karl Marx about a value-full position. Weber argues very simply: we have to recognize what our values are; our responsibilities as thinkers and educators are to focus on our values, to be articulate about them, and to make them clear to our colleagues and those with whom we would argue so that they understand who we are, what we believe in, and where we are trying to lead them; and, given this information, others can respond accordingly.

That is, for the lack of a better term, a value-full position, and that's not new with Max Weber.

The French Positivists did the same thing when they talked about making society a better place by engineering it. DeLesseps was a Positivist, and the concept of the Suez Canal came directly out of this philosophy.

Look back to Plato when he argued values in the Republic. He went a bit further than I would go, because through analogy he places societal value on people, distinguishing between gold, silver, and bronze. We might think about those categories as castes. Overstating his position that "those who know should rule," the rulers are likened to gold. Then there are the functionaries, who are likened to silver. The majority of workers are viewed as the base metal of society, and they are likened to bronze.

Going back further, the Old Testament is full of values. The Ten Commandments are a set of values. And the Hammurabic Code, which predates them, is a basic value system. It says that whatever you're going to do to me, I'm going to do back to you—"an eye for an eye." Interestingly, that statement is what was later turned into "do not do that unto others which you would not have done unto you," what most of us know as the Golden Rule.

These are all value statements. They are still with us. They reflect the main thrust of American culture, and, as such, they reflect the value systems with which our students come to us.

Value Themes

In *Habits of the Heart* (1986), Robert Bellah and his colleagues identify four value-system themes for American culture. An effective strategic plan that has a real impact on the community we serve cannot be successful unless all of these value themes are present. They have to be recognized and then responded to.

The first is the earliest in our history, the biblical/religious theme. The second is a republican theme (not the Republican Party, but, rather, republicanism as represented in Jeffersonian democracy). The third theme is managerial, part and parcel of the Industrial Revolution in this country. The fourth theme, the most recent, is the therapeutic. It is the theme that has been stated as ''I'm OK, you're OK.''

Each theme has five dimensions: a basis for action; a cultural imperative; a control mechanism; a primary social institution; and a primary economic institution or structure (see Figure 1). By reviewing these dimensions we can look at how these themes are manifested in today's culture.

Figure 1. Some Dimensions of Major Themes in Contemporary American Culture.

Theme	Basis for Action	Cultural Imperative	Control Mechanism	Primary School Institution	Primary Economic Institution
Biblical/ Religious	Religious Group	Morality	Shame	The Church	Tribe/Extended Family
Republican (Jeffersonian Democracy)	Geographic Group	Ethics	Justice in Law	The State	Community
Managerial	Utilitarian Individualism	Productivity	Distributive Justice	The Company	Trade and Industry Corporations
Therapeutic	Expressive Individualism	Self-Actualization	Guilt	Self	Small Business Services/Nuclear Family

Regarding their basis for action, the first two themes are group themes relying on either the religious group experience or the community group experience. The last two themes are individual themes. They are what de Tocqueville recognized in *Democracy in America* as the utilitarian individual (managerial) theme and the expressive individual (therapeutic) theme.

In terms of the cultural imperative related to each theme, the biblical/religious theme's cultural imperative is morality. The community political action theme, or republican theme, deals with ethics. The managerial theme deals with productivity, or the economic imperative. The therapeutic theme deals with personal satisfaction and personal development—in other words, self-actualization.

In terms of control mechanisms, the biblical/religious theme looks at shame. The republican theme looks at justice administered by law. The managerial theme also looks at justice, but from a different perspective. It talks about distributive justice, the distribution of goods and services and how those accrue to you, me, or our group. It talks about who gets what in the system, and why, and under what conditions. The control mechanism for the therapeutic theme is self-growth with honesty and, ultimately, freedom, or guilt for failure to achieve.

The primary social institution for the biblical/religious theme is the church; for republicanism, the state; for the managerial theme, the company; for the therapeutic theme, the self—an internalized structure.

The primary economic institution or structure for the biblical/religious theme is the tribe or extended family. For the republican theme, it's the community. For the managerial theme, it's trade and industrial corporations. And for the therapeutic theme, it's services and small business, in the contemporary sense of delivering services.

What does all of this have to do with strategic planning?

If, in strategic planning, you only develop a plan, in my judgment you've failed. If you make a nice document, put it on the shelf and say, "Here's our plan," you've failed. That's not the objective. If, on the other hand, you implement processes that allow goals and objectives to be achieved, which allows you to go from A to B to C, and you incorporate an interactive environment in that approach, then I believe you'll be doing what the Japanese have done with their quality circles and now what successful American corporations are adopting.

The secret of the Japanese quality circle model is no secret at all. It is, in fact, the four cultural themes identified in *Habits of the Heart* integrated into one small social system. All members of the quality circle have a moral imperative to support their co-workers. They have to be ethical in their behavior. They have to be productive and achieve group outcomes. And they are expected to attain personal satisfaction in the process.

That's the hot model, and we've had it all along. They simply borrowed it from us. But, instead of splintering the four themes, the Japanese put them together.

Some External Influences

State government is not going to be neutral about what we do, nor is it going to be neutral about the values we are allowed to hold as institutions.

California's master plan for postsecondary education has a title that is a value statement. It is *California Faces*. . . (yellow, black, brown, pink) *California's Future: Education for Citizenship in a Multi-Cultural Democracy*.

That's about as pointed a title, in terms of the value statement in those words, as you can possibly write. It's an affirmative action document in the best sense of affirmative action. It is a statement about taking action affirmatively, for producing an effective education system in the most culturally pluralistic state in this nation. As an example, there are eighty-three different native languages being spoken in the Los Angeles public schools.

In this document, after the philosophy and value statements are made, there follows page after page after page of action recommendations. A good college planning team should follow this model and concentrate on action.

In addition to the questions of race and ethnicity, and whether we can integrate ourselves into a society rather than a number of small foreign countries that exist side by side, we are going to have to face a series of counter-trends.

First, there has been a lot of talk about high touch, since community colleges are often into the high tech business and must not forget about the human side. I want to tell you that high touch is a sham—no state government is interested in funding it, even though that's what they may say.

What government is interested in is accountability. The emphasis on student services is to make sure that you do what they want you to do, when they want you to do it. That is what the assessment programs are all about, and that's what the follow-up programs are all about. Your challenge is going to be to translate that, and to make it something that is educationally viable in your district.

A second counter-trend that goes along with accountability is recentralization. Most state governments will be willing to give you more money to run your institutions provided you're willing to bite the bullet and have a statewide system of community colleges. That kind of move may not be palatable to everyone, but it's a trend we can't ignore.

A third counter-trend is the new familialism. You see this counter-trend all around you. You see younger people now talking about permanent relationships, about personal relationships that are family-oriented. These values are back in vogue; the whole concept, then, of how you create this family environment in your work life, in your education, in driving your automobile back and forth to work, is one that we have to deal with. It is there as a newly emerging, underlying theme.

We can take advantage of the new familialism with a kind of statistical paternalism, something that combines high tech and high touch. We're going to have magic in the form of assessment tests. We will have to be able to predict how our students are going to do in order to place them and in order to evaluate whether our curricular offerings are having the right impact. We will be able to offer our students highly accurate guidance counseling, to the point that the college will become a helpful parent to the student.

We Need Style

In order to achieve our values, our colleges must have their commitments supported by style.

Any place you ever dream about, any place you have been that was memorable, remains memorable because it has style.

Community colleges have style if they possess the following four attributes:

• A consensus shared by all members of the college community about what the college is, about its mission, its goals and objectives, and about how and by whom the mission, goals, and objectives will be realized. I'm not saying that everybody's going to dot every "i" and cross every "t" the same way, but I'll bet you that a shared consensus on mission, goals, and objectives exists.

• They know who their students are and they know why those students come to the college. They know what their students want to accomplish while they're at the college. They know something about how effective the college has been in enabling students to accomplish those objectives.

• The college leadership shares a vision about what the college should be and how it can be all that it should.

• They know how to reach out to prospective students. Their staffs don't say things like "We've never done that," or "We tried that twenty years ago and it didn't work." On the contrary, the staff is willing to do whatever it takes to get the job done. Avoiding the consequences is not part of the college staff's vocabulary. They simply roll up their sleeves and do it.

Getting It Done

Unlike goal values, process values are those activities, approaches, strategies, and tactics that we adopt to reach our objectives. In our organizations, these process values generally take one of two forms—compliance or accountability.

Compliance systems are structured by prescriptions and proscriptions. You are told exactly what you must do, and you are told exactly what you must not do. States love to do that. Then if you don't do as you are told, if you deviate, they withhold funding or express displeasure in some other way, such as enacting more stringent legislation.

Accountability systems, on the other hand, are structured to accomplish outcomes and results. They are oriented toward goals and objectives. Rather than punishing failure, they reward success.

Figure 2 contrasts some of the differences between compliance systems and accountability systems.

The characteristics of accountability systems listed in Figure 2 are not unlike the characteristics of America's best-run companies, as identified by Peters and Waterman (1982). Figure 3 presents an abstract of these characteristics.

If we compare Figures 2 and 3, it seems clear that systems of accountability and systems of excellence share the same fundamental bias for action and change based on processes that allow for differences among participants; tolerate failure and reward success; promote autonomy, entrepreneurship, and initiative; share information; and seek objectives that are meaningful to those involved.

Figure 2. Characteristic Differences Between Compliance Systems and Accountability Systems.

Compliance Systems	Accountability Systems
Structured via prescriptions and proscriptions	Structured to accomplish outcomes and results
Controls-oriented	Goals- and objectives-oriented
Promotes status quo	Promotes change
Does not accept ambiguous results	Views ambiguity as a positive force for change
Promotes inclusive management	Promotes management by exception
• Hierarchical control	• Network coordination
• Top-down	• Field-based
• Delegates responsibility	• Delegates authority
• Creates rules and expects them to be followed	• Creates processes to promote participation and involvement
• Punishes failure	• Rewards accomplishments
• Views the system as closed	• Views the system as open and fluid
Uses reporting systems	Uses information systems
• Is descriptive	• Is analytical
• Focuses on rules	• Focuses on issues and problems
• Relies on data	• Uses information
• Seeks minutia	• Seeks trends
• Restricts access to data	• Makes information available
• Data out-of-date as rules change	• Information is futures-oriented; its currency is independent of time

Revised by previous publication by the author. "The Other Side of Assessment." In D. Bray & M. Belcher, (Eds.), *Issues in Student Assessment,* New Directions for Community Colleges Series, No. 59. San Francisco: Jossey-Bass, 1987, p. 18.

Comparison of the two lists also makes it clear that the characteristics of compliance systems are in direct conflict with the characteristics of America's best-run companies. Where accountability systems seek and promote excellence, compliance systems develop and implement minimum standards. In short, where accountability systems engage individuals, and hence their institutions, to do and be all that they can do and be, compliance systems demand that individuals and their institutions do and be what they are told to do and be—no more and no less.

Image

In order to implement our values, we have to convince other people that we are worthy. That means we have to market our image—not our programs, not our services, but our image.

We have to project an image that's responsible and successful. We can't go around saying, "Woe is us, we have no money." We can't go around saying, "If only you guys would do this, we could be great." We have to be

Figure 3. Characteristics of America's Best-Run Companies.

- A bias for action
- Organizational fluidity

- Customer orientation

- Empowers employees
- Fewer managers, more operators
- Insistence on employee-based initiative
- Good leadership, not overly managed
- Intense communication systems

- Promotes experimentation
- Promotes autonomy and entrepreneurship among employees
- Tailors products and services to the customer base
- Tolerates failure
- "Don't Write Reports. Do It"
- Objectives that are meaningful to employees
- Views structure as an extended family
- Focuses on priorities supported by shared values

Source: Peters and Waterman, 1982, p. 18.

great despite what others may be doing, and then say, "You want us to be greater, give us A, B, C, D, E."

Legislators respond to that. They do not respond to "Woe is me."

Legislators also do not like eighty-two different choruses being sung simultaneously. We have to deliver our message with a focused, singular voice.

If you've ever thought, "Well I know how to make this happen, I'll just call the newspaper and tell them what's going on," know that that's the best way to guarantee mediocrity for your institution, now and for the future. The best way to not serve your community is to wash your laundry in public.

The University of California is arguably the most successful public education institution in the world. It has an $8 billion-plus annual operating budget, $6 billion of which is its own money. When University of California representatives disagree, they argue behind closed doors. When they go to the press, they say, "This is what the University of California says." The University projects a responsible and successful image for itself.

One last point. In planning for 2000, the American community college has its greatest opportunity ever: a chance to re-create our colleges. We have the opportunity to review everything, keep what we like, and replace what we don't like.

As you do that, please keep this in mind: we cannot simply run around sloganeering and then not deliver. To be accountable in the process we have to be what we say we are.

Peter M. Hirsch is associate dean at Portland Community College in Portland, Oregon.

CHAPTER SEVEN

Successful Linkages

By David Ponitz

COMMUNITY COLLEGES ACROSS the country need to develop a more accurate focus on the potential linkages that will help serve a broader spectrum of students. Linkages represent a planning dimension that addresses some of the dramatic changes in American values and the changing demographics within our society. We discuss these changes intellectually as community college people, but many times we really don't understand how they affect our commitment and our classroom.

Linkages require us to seek a greater degree of partnership and cooperation with increasingly diverse external constituencies. Linkages require us to be more creative and adaptable as we work in consort with community organizations. Linkages can also create wonderful opportunities for our students to integrate their formal educational experiences in nontraditional ways outside the college. They also provide a means of keeping the administration, faculty, and staff in touch with the external marketplace.

Each institution is attracted to potential linkages for different reasons. Regardless of the reasons, institutions should avoid the temptation to "link" with everyone. The linkages pursued must be compatible with the institutional mission and must yield some concrete, long-term benefits. The question that educators should ask is whether the linkage leads to more effective education.

Community colleges have formed linkages that concur with organizational traditions and values. As times have changed, these values and traditions have changed. The decade of the 1990s will bring about even more changes. It is important to examine some of the societal changes that work to improve or detract from our opportunities for successful linkages. These trends seem to capture the personality of our time in history. These trends also reflect the personality of those that we serve as we attempt to establish successful linkages.

Changing Times

Many of our value changes are related to differences in economics. A lot of us are products of Great Depression parents who talked about self-denial ethics, bringing us up with gems of wisdom like: "You live a clean life, save your money, and eventually in heaven you'll get your reward." New values of self-fulfillment have certainly replaced that view.

Concurrent with the change from self-denial to self-fulfillment has come the knowledge that though we talk about higher standards of living, for the first time we're saying to our kids that they probably will not have a higher standard of living than we have now. Our children in turn are answering that maybe there are other dimensions to life beyond the acquisition of things. They aren't going to try to keep up with the Joneses, but they are going to define what a better quality of life means. The definition of success by dollars, home size, or model of car is not workable for them.

Values are also being altered because of the speed of change. We're in a "now" generation. David Packard of Hewlett-Packard said that all of his company's products are researched and marketed in a three-year period of time . . . right now! We are in a fast-moving era that requires flexibility, adaptability to change, and new ways of thinking, as we hear young people talk about opportunities that were not thought very much about just a few decades ago.

Some values are being altered because of changes in gender roles. Everybody knew whose job it was to make the bed or take out the garbage when gender roles were traditional. Now it is very blurred and rightly so! A friend said to me not long ago, "My wife and I have a contract about the assignment of work in our home. I think I am being slighted because I've got to do more work around the house than my wife. We both work so I'm going to go home this weekend and change the contract in terms of my workload."

I saw him several weeks later and asked how it was going. He said, "I struck out—my wife was unwilling to change the contract." Six months later they divorced. The point of this story is merely to show how an approach to marriage and its responsibilities can differ from one generation to the next, not to suggest that shared home responsibilities lead to incompatibility!

Changes in gender roles have brought new value dimensions to the interpretation of families. We have gone beyond the Norman Rockwell family of mom and dad and two kids, which now makes up only about 7 percent of the population.

There are all kinds of alternative lifestyles and alternative families, and they raise a number of complex, value-driven questions. Should same-sex partners get the benefits that a typical marriage provides? What are the special dimensions of a "househusband" family? What impact will child care have on children who from the age of a few weeks have been cared for by someone other than the parents? How is the decline in leisure time impacting family relationships? What is the future for children of teen parents or for those young parents themselves? What is the impact of delayed child-bearing on career couples?

Many of these differing views get in the way of middle-class people with traditional middle-class values. They also get in the way of how we deal with our students and their questions, especially as they may conflict with our own cultural biases.

My son, a recent college graduate, was complaining that for a couple of weeks on his new job, even though he was paid over-time, he had to work seventy hours a week. When I replied that working seventy hours a week was fairly common, he responded, "Well, I've got so many other things to do!" Perhaps our views differ because a lot of my generation live to work, whereas we must assume that many of our students work to live. That may sound like a catchy phrase, but it really begins to describe how a lot of people view life. It is unlikely that our students will apply a Puritan work ethic to their studies. Many of today's students will view their educational training in short-term segments, while accepting attainment in small increments over time.

Other value differences have to do with pluralism. An earlier generation read *Life* magazine, largely because we wanted to see what people and other geographic regions looked like. We aspired to be like them, to look like them, live like them. Magazines like *Life, Colliers,* and the *Saturday Evening Post* are not around anymore; instead we have highly individualized magazine markets targeted to highly specialized groups who enjoy that niche. We are bombarded with products and reading materials that celebrate cultural diversity as well, and we recognize the importance of these kinds of learning.

Coupled with this change is a lessening of nationalism. We used to know that when the president made a statement on foreign policy, everybody got behind it and agreed. Certainly that is not true now, as noted by recent addresses of President Bush. We've become less nationalistic because we know more about the world. Due to our new pluralism, we talk about all kinds of different approaches to domestic and international issues.

How do value changes and more pluralistic attitudes affect us in the community colleges? Most organizations go through certain life cycles. They go through birth and they go through growth. Most of us who have been in the field for a long time like to talk about doubling enrollments every year for five years, or make statements like, "I've been there fifteen years and our enrollment has tripled." But the fact is that a lot of institutions are now in a state of maturity. Although some colleges have experienced some interesting growth in numbers, the maturity of their ideas may be what we need to be carefully thinking about. The real trick is to figure out how to move from maturity to rebirth without going through decline!

Many colleges across this country are in decline because faculty members and administrators are not willing to address the new kinds of students. Students whose values confront our values or whose beliefs are very different from our own have unique needs for new faculty-student relationships. Colleges that are not meeting these new demands may have a president who is a technocrat or a board that is unwilling to look at the changes in values and demographics. Perhaps we should add another "C" to our name and become Contemporary Community Colleges, implying flexibility and adaptability!

Elements of renewal cannot be automated in order to bring a sense of currency to the campus. They need intensive study, more study than just going through a casual one-shot committee. Organizational and individual development is difficult to achieve. Presidents and faculty members know that the choice of study committee members can determine whether or not the ideas will proceed or die. We all know that change can take a long time and that committee members can delay a process or water down an idea so much that the impact on students and staff will not make a real difference. If we want organizational rebirth we must plan for it and work at achieving it with a sense of focus and unity—president, board, faculty, and staff together.

Someone once said that we like to look at the community college as a marathon. Perhaps today we should look at it like a cross-country race or a steeplechase, with ever-changing terrain and challenges. Before deregulation, Bell Telephone Company thought everything would be the same. Then all of a sudden, it found it had to "sprint" to keep up with competition and with changing technology. How do we sprint to keep up with changing needs and new approaches?

People once talked about hours and days, and now people talk about nanoseconds. Things need to move rapidly, to pop, to get done. This is a society that puts emphasis on speed and moving and acting quickly. We're moving from everything being predictable to many things being very ambiguous and speeding by us with great rapidity.

How do we live in a world of ambiguity? We know that for many administrators this can be a very difficult condition. How do you keep all the balls up in the air at the same time and still make things happen? What are the important responses that administrators must make?

In the past community colleges talked about market share. We don't talk about that anymore. Now we must deal with market creation. What are new student markets? What are the student markets that we need to create? Take a look at the nation's newspapers on any given morning. Is there a market for helping people who may be out of work as a result of the closing of a military facility or a reduction in the work force of a factory or business? Is there a new organization, perhaps with an international genesis, starting in a small nearby community? We need to think about the possibility of linkages like this and be ever alert to changes within our community that are our responsibility and that could create new student markets.

We still like mass marketing because of the comfort of doing what we have always done; after all, community colleges are all about a mass market. We have liberal arts and occupational programs, staff development, and community education. We don't have a single niche. We have multiple niches in order to serve our diversity of students.

We also know that we are stewards of change. We give major lip service to educating for change, but to really accomplish a substantive difference in our colleges is a very large challenge. For instance, how do we go from the Frederick Taylor concept of management, which broke job training down into repetitive skills and which was based on early twentieth century values and a much stronger sense of rationalism, to the organizational reality of the last decade of the twentieth century? If we ask an employee to be responsible for quality control, the employee is likely to reply, "Who me?" We have to be responsible for figuring out with a group of people the kind of work ethic that will be necessary to put a product together that is responsive to a new mass of students. "Who, me?" becomes "Yes, you." You've got to help figure out how to do a better job and build a better product.

Recently Tom Peters said that Japanese companies have thirty suggestions per employee in their suggestion box. The number of suggestions from American workers to improve their own performance is 0.14 per year. This gives you some idea of quality control emphasis in the two cultures. The Japanese accept 65 percent of the suggestions they receive. They are moving from a work force equipped to work only with muscle to an employee group involved in continuous learning, from concentrated power to dispersed power with lots of people making decisions and participating in the process.

The very steep organizational pyramid formerly used by most organizations does not work as well anymore. Most community college organizations are flat structures because candidly those in the management team on the firing line who are involved with students are in a better position to make decisions than the president. But we have to continue to be willing to accept opportunities to disperse power. Our power configuration is changing from a central mainframe computer mentality to a network of PCs. This produces added energy, added information, and reduced isolation. The former concept of working in one department and being disinterested in another department is a sentiment whose time has passed.

When I worked with a large Midwest university several years ago, I introduced two full professors in psychology who didn't know one another. Both of them had been there fifteen years. Isolation versus integration. Isolation versus working together, networking and linking, trying to figure out what kind of skills can be shared in conjunctive efforts to make them more effective. If we don't have that kind of integration or are not willing to pool skills, we probably aren't going to solve many of these major problems we face. We certainly won't be able to respond to new markets and the students who comprise them.

Another of our outmoded concepts is that if we can't change anything we should just keep it safe and sound. But a safe and sound approach to curriculum and students is likely to create rebellion. I read an interesting story about how, at one of the great research universities in the world, one morning undergraduate students stood up and complained, "Damn it! Our classes have got 500 students in them. We aren't going to take this anymore." Students appear to be much more fragile than they were just five years ago and need a lot more help. They need more counseling, more tutorial services, and more visual learning opportunities.

Our society's demographics of aging present another opportunity. Approximately 10,000 people reach the age of forty each day. Only about 8,000 people become teenagers, while the fastest-growing segment of our population is the cohort of people over seventy-five. What implications do these figures have for potential student populations? How consistent is your community with these general statistics? What is the impact of certain microsegments of the population on the marketplace and on training?

Another current trend of interest to us is the privatization movement, in which various groups are trying to do the jobs of certain governmental units in a more efficient and effective way. Why is it that government has placed the operation of prisons, fire and police departments, and the garbage business in private hands? Why is it that governors have become heads of educational groups? Because they are saying, "Look, you folks tell too many war stories. You don't get down to the guts of the matter. Students come out of your educational institutions with no value added. We can do better than you can." There is more to come if we don't get busy!

Recently I had a discussion with a major computer group about the typical teaching load of a faculty member. I said that our faculty members are on the podium thirty hours a week—that is, they are teaching thirty hours a week and have Friday afternoons off to prepare for next week. Company officials responded that they could do that kind of job more effectively and efficiently. We like to turn our backs on assaults like this and say we're the best teaching group, but these kinds of challenges are happening in every state in the union.

Consumerism is another movement of current importance. Some colleges have told employers, "We guarantee our students. If they graduate with an associate degree, and they don't meet your needs, send them back and we'll retrain them free, because we haven't done our job." Faculty response to such a challenge could well bring about a positive solution to consumer needs.

Another important factor has to do with the role of women and their increasing importance in the work force. Seventy-five percent of all new entrants to the work force will be women and ethnic minorities. How are we planning to respond to this? Women are coming to our campuses with concussive force. They are good students and committed to their education. We need to provide them opportunities different from what many traditional students need; they are a new market that requires a new response.

Many other developments on the horizon require us to be on the cutting edge of new technology and developments. Scientific accomplishments like gene splicing, global free trade, a united Europe, and environmental issues as they relate to fragile economies of Third World countries all offer potential for the community college movement to be a catalyst for helping people understand and adapt to dramatic societal change.

We live in a dynamic world environment. These illustrations of change are likely to be altered again and again. Our capacity to adapt to external changes, regardless of whether they are organizational or individual, and our willingness to keep in touch by seeking valuable linkages should be part of the pathway to community college success in the decade ahead.

The How and Why of Linkage

Linkages should be pursued because they may well make the vital difference as to whether a community has a viable work force and whether people will be able to adapt to dramatic changes around them. The "how to" has no set formula. Viable linkages will change from circumstance to circumstance. How we establish a successful linkage is tied to an institutional desire to create a win-win situation with another organization. The potential for a successful linkage can be found almost anywhere in each community. We need not look further than the public schools, business, industry, public agencies, state government, prison systems, unions, proprietary educators, and local government. Most of us have an ongoing linkage with the federal government through student financial aid and other grant programs.

If community college leaders are creative and look at institutional linkages, they will find that usually a formal or informal needs assessment was done and people began communicating about sharing resources and working together on common problems. Local program advisory committees are keys to helping a college know exactly what its students need. Reach out to them—those wonderful volunteers who have one foot in the real world and one in academe. They can tell us what our students need to know and need to be able to do.

Linkages can credential the college to members of the community who might not otherwise interact with it. Linkages create a positive image for the institution. When community colleges establish cooperative programming with other organizations, they improve their public relations base in the community. This P.R. support in turn helps to solidify the fiscal and psychological relationship the college must have with the community.

When community colleges explore the significant opportunities that linkages afford they can reasonably expect some of the following results:

- Knowledge that they have been responsive to baseline community needs
- Enthusiasm directed at the institution from external organizations
- An opportunity for shared planning that derives from shared values and beliefs
- A chance to pool resources, especially financial resources
- New opportunities for additional linkages as the word spreads about the institution's capacity to respond to baseline community needs
- The networking value of working with superintendents, mayors, city managers, community developers, and others whose support the college will continue to need
- Developing new relationships with local constituents

51

Let's examine some of the possible linkages that are already working. One dramatic example is a community college that signed a $1 million contract to train 4,200 people (every person in one plant) over a three-year period about world competitive markets. Another college has developed a training contract with a union under which all of its members will take a special course in personal finance. This was done because the union membership had so many problems with people not being able to handle their financial responsibilities and getting into great difficulty in their personal lives, which intruded on their work and hence the quality of the company's product.

In many examples like this, factory employees build faith and trust in the educational system and move from labor studies or personal finance courses to courses in computer science or engineering technology so they can do a better job in their particular work area. Remember, for the most part, these are blue-collar workers who don't have a college education. We have to keep in mind that 75 percent of all the job categories by the year 1995 are going to need some education beyond high school. The job market is creating our student market!

Experience has demonstrated that many times community college faculties can do a much better teaching job than the four-year university faculties. Our faculties have better ideas, but we need to present them, sometimes working in tandem with universities on research opportunities or a host of other mutually beneficial projects. There is no need to wait for the grand, big university to make the proposal; when we have an idea, we should make a proposal, involve the university, and work through the legislative process. The articulation opportunities between the community colleges, high schools, and four-year universities are unbelievable. The opportunities and the dollars are there for these linkages.

Another excellent area for cooperation is in the area of international education. Opportunities are there to support faculties and staff knowledgeable about the global village. That means a link stronger than a textbook. Global education has to be integrated throughout each institution's endeavors. Many times our students have had more international travel opportunities than our faculty members. We must strive to provide exchange opportunity links for faculty, special courses abroad for students, special in-class experiences with international business persons, training and skill acquisition in appropriate cultural behavior, and, above all, opportunity for acquiring second language skills.

There is a truism that education equals change, and that if one does not change, one dies. What is the role of faculty involvement in this change? If faculty teach their x number of hours and meet their specified students for counseling, should more be expected of them? Candidly, we must say that much more is expected. They are doing our students no favor if they are unwilling to go the extra mile to change, to be involved with all the necessary linkages that will deal with our great student diversity.

The truly great community college is involved in the hopes, the dreams, and the aspirations of its people. It must serve as a vehicle to help students resolve their frustrations and assist them in their individual problem solving. There's no longer a neat, wonderful barrier between the town and the gown, the brick wall and the ivy. Some colleges may not have the brick wall anymore, but they may put up a psychological barrier that can be even more pervasive and dangerous.

Our values are changing and they will continue to change. Our society is on the fast track. We must change our institutional values and respond to changing demographics or we will render our students ineffective in a world that grows more complex every day. We must tear down old monuments that marked our organizations in the past. We must change our thinking about gathering students into our systems and how we should educate them after they arrive. We should be energetic in our pursuit of linkages that will enable us to serve those who may be outside the traditional system but need our help.

This is our challenge for today and the near future. Our work toward improving links between the college and the community will involve a combination of creativity, entrepreneurship, and service. It will also require time and effort—and the will to do it.

David Ponitz is president of Sinclair Community College in Dayton, Ohio.

CHAPTER EIGHT

Collaboration Within the College

By Jerry Sue Owens

THE AMERICAN ASSOCIATION of Community and Junior Colleges (AACJC) has focused on partnerships. AACJC President Dale Parnell has been an advocate of partnerships between high schools and community colleges and universities. So, for the last year, I have been giving much thought to partnerships and collaboration within institutions and among institutions because collegial collaboration is very important. It occurred to me that I needed to know much more about student services, continuing education, and areas of community college work other than my field of instruction.

Partnerships and information about what each college unit is doing become very helpful as we problem-solve. There is great value in collaborative work and cooperative evaluation as opposed to trying to solve problems in isolation. We usually think about collaboration and community in an external institutional context. I would like for us to think about communication and collaboration within our own institutions. Collaboration is not always easy because there are territories and turfdoms that shrink instead of broaden the relationship that allows us to share the knowledge and expertise that we have within our institutions.

We find that many schools are having to do as much as they can to increase their enrollments. When we look at recruiting students, we are faced with an increase of nontraditional students who are for the first time taking advantage of community college education. That creates a new scenario in terms of what units within the college must do to work together.

We are increasing student enrollment through recruiting marketing and public relations. Many of the new students have not had previous college experience or may not be well prepared for postsecondary education. Many administrators in community colleges were not trained to deal with the issues that face us these days, and this complicates our efforts to assist faculty in campus-based collaborative endeavors to make their jobs more effective and productive.

Many of the students who are coming to us fit into the category of "high risk." We are doing as many things as we can to retain students and to retain our own sanity as we work with these students. They exact a heavy price. They are challenging; they are fun; and they are very rewarding. As educators we have to continually think about our capacity to keep giving and yet renew our spirit and keep our own morale up so that we continue doing a good job.

Many challenges interfere with our spirit, such as entry-level and outcome assessments and quality in the curriculum. All of us are looking for ways to make the content more meaningful, interesting, and dynamic in order to meet the needs of our students.

Faculty renewal and development become very important as we look at a maturing faculty. I made that comment to my faculty recently, and one man raised his hand and said, "You mean I'm getting older." Yes, we all are maturing in this business because most of us have been in it for a long time. There is a need for constant development and renewal of goals for each of us. We need a way to reaffirm that we are on the right track and that other people are learning as much from what we are doing as we are learning from them.

Another area of concern should be student retention. How can we retain students at our institutions longer, not just for the sake of maintaining and retaining, but because we know how valuable their education will be in the workplace and to their future success? It is not going to be enough just to be trained; people are going to need to be cross-trained and cross-educated in order to maximize their skills. We as educators know what they need. Our purpose is to give them as much education as possible while they are with us.

We need to keep them interested and keep them in college. Cultural diversity certainly became a buzzword of the '80s and continues into the '90s. We are seeing more diversity among the college-bound. How we accommodate, appreciate, and value the differences among people is a major challenge. The climate of acceptance and tolerance will be instrumental in nontraditional student survival.

Higher educational opportunity has been greatly impacted by financial aid. Many of our students are becoming discouraged by having to obtain loans and accumulate heavy debt instead of receiving grants while in college. And, if you are conscious at all about what it costs to attend college (and the books are almost as costly as tuition), you know the dilemma that students are facing with financial aid.

Child care is another major issue for higher education today. For those people who are trying to go to school and raise a family, child care becomes very important. The dilemma for many of us is finding the space for child care on our campuses. We need classrooms and learning labs, and yet we are restructuring our facilities in order to provide some form of child care. These issues create some new decision-making dimensions for us.

When I taught sixth grade many years ago, "new math" was just being developed. I am not sure that any of us ever quite understood new math! As I stayed a chapter ahead of the students, I finally realized the problem—I was trying to do new math with an "old math" mind. And as I think of what we sometimes are doing in community colleges, we are teaching new, nontraditional students with a very traditional educational philosophy.

And so the challenge for us is to begin to rethink what we know. How can we restate and rephrase what we teach for a new type of student? I'm not saying that traditional content is invalid. But can we restructure it and present it so that the students are excited and motivated and it fits their learning pattern and learning style?

I discovered from my former teaching experience that I needed to rethink the new math and the old math. While the content may be the same and very valid, I had to rethink delivery. As we consider the new students who are coming to us, we get a sense of the bell-shaped curve and what that means. Those students who are on the front row will always be there, and they're always going to take from us—they learn in spite of the professor. The ones on the back row need us more; they are the ones that we're trying to keep awake or trying to wake up.

Many students are striving very hard to reach difficult goals. Several of our students have heard the words, "Judging by your school records and your aptitude tests, I'd say graduation would be a bad career move for you." Many of our students have heard those words in high school, junior high, and grade school, and so we are now saying in community colleges, "It's not a bad career move. There is an opportunity for you, and we're going to take all of the resources of this community college to help you to attain your career goal."

In Minnesota, when we were getting ready for final exams, one student said, "I've got a test in English and history today. There's never a blizzard around when you need one." In Minnesota, they're often praying for blizzards around the time for final exams. I never have to check the schedule when it's final exam time—I just look at the strained faces in the hallway, and I know that many people are thinking that they should have studied harder and studied longer.

Students let us know that final exams always come at a bad time. Summer school comes at a really bad time too! For many of our students, most of what we're trying to do comes at a really bad time, especially since they are trying to work and take care of their families. They are so stretched that it is difficult to get an education and participate in the activities and programs that make an educational experience special.

As educators we need to develop a broader vision of what we are doing than what we see in our own unit, our own area, and our own world within the community college. How can we broaden that vision so that there is an appreciation in the academic area for what the counselor is doing, and there is an appreciation in the business office for what the registrar is doing? That collaboration and understanding of different kinds of jobs within the community college helps broaden the perspective and appreciation for what is within an institution as we all move toward the goal of educating our students. It is sometimes very difficult to remove ourselves from a narrow niche.

Our students know some things as well as we do. They say, "Word has it that the world is in pretty rough shape—pass it on." With the many issues that we face in community colleges today, it is a pretty rough place. With the limited resources that all of us have, it is a tough challenge to try to accomplish our goals in a finite period of time. Most of us are trying to do more with less. And this is going to be a theme for the future of community colleges nationally.

If you look at the current population as the financiers of education in the form of taxes, it is clear that there is resistance to spending. No one really wants to pay more taxes.

We can make our best case. We can tell our stories—and they are good stories—but they are very difficult stories for people who are looking at increased health care and retirement costs in relation to putting more dollars into education. We are going to be forced to be more creative and to maximize limited resources.

An excellent book by Rosa Beth Moss-Kantor, *When Giants Learn to Dance*, describes how large corporations are facing many of the same kinds of challenges. The book examines how corporations need to do more with less and maximize their efficiency because of international competition. She endorses the collaboration among major corporations like IBM and 3M. Instead of each one being an independent corporation doing everything on their own, they are going to have to look more at capitalizing on each other's resources and putting that combined power to work.

One reason why we in community colleges must collaborate is that many of our students are sailboats instead of luxury liners. They need so much more in order to get underway. Many of the students who go to universities are luxury liners, and no matter what the professor does, they are going to succeed. They are not going to capsize. But with our typical students, the least little thing that occurs within the institution discourages them and they stop out.

We also need to consider some of the major questions facing higher education. Sometimes the questions are so difficult and complex we would rather not even consider them.

A little girl was asked by her teacher to name the king whose daughter's marriage made possible the unification of Denmark and Norway in 1380. The student said, "Wow, that's the kind of question that makes your temples throb. It makes your ears ring and your hair stand on end. It makes your eyes water and your cheeks burn, your mouth turn dry and teeth ache. A question like that can destroy your whole head."

When we think of the magnitude of the educational task, just asking the difficult questions of our time can destroy our whole head.

So the problem for us is making sure that we ask ourselves the right questions as we begin to collaborate and cooperate within our institutions and work more productively. But I think as any good test giver knows, life is not just a series of true and false questions. How do we change our programs and services from true and false questions? How do we create options—multiple choices—for our students?

Successful programs generally have broad characteristics that have meaning to many different people. We have to ensure that our programs and services are comprehensive and are broadly accepted throughout the institution.

We know within our own units and departments the difficulties of collaboration. We have some definite ideas about what it is like to work with committees. If I say, "Off with his head," someone answers, "Ahh yes, and we'll need a task force to decide how and when to do it. I have here a list of sixty-three people and twenty-seven departments to be consulted."

So oftentimes in our decision making we have learned that it is easier and faster if one or two people or if a single department makes a decision. But it may not necessarily be the best decision. Sometimes if we work collaboratively on a decision, the benefits are enhanced because of the diverse input resulting in ownership. In collaborative efforts, there really is no one who is more equal than another. It is a simple matter of trying to put the issues on the table and seeing who has the best response for that particular problem. If we are interested in collaboration and the successful decision making that can result from it, then we must consider maximizing the idea of power.

Collaboration can be effectively illustrated by viewing each of us in an orchestra playing instruments. We can all play the same tune, or we can all play our own instruments, each to a different beat. With collaboration, we will be playing the same tune. Everyone in a community college would be committed.

Partnership through collaboration may mean looking at services to our students in a more comprehensive manner. I have worked on accreditation evaluation teams with some schools where collaboration did not occur. People saw themselves as little islands doing their own thing. Given the needs of our students today, we need to know everything about each unit so that we can help each other understand the students' needs better. The collaborative model of student services simply suggests an overlapping of what we are doing and an opportunity to help one another understand what is happening in our divisions and in our own work areas. Even better, and this is much tougher, with institutional collaboration we bring all forces together around an issue. Public relations, student services, academic affairs, and finance are just a few units that can benefit from institutionwide collaboration.

A major national issue that affects the entire institution is the issue of assessment of basic skills. What is needed? What reading level is important for history, for psychology, for chemistry? A review of the content of a course and textbook readability must be made regarding skills necessary for successful course completion. It is not enough to leave that task for the student service staff.

When I first began my tenure as president, we had exit tests before graduation. All students had to pass a test in English, reading, and math before they could graduate. However, we did not have entry-level testing.

It seemed to me that we were beginning at the end. We were willing to say to the world, "This is what the student knows," but we did not know what they knew when they arrived or the value added. We had to rethink entry-level testing. We also had to take a look at what we were doing with developmental education. Did we have adequate levels of reading, writing, and math courses to satisfy student needs? In fact, we didn't.

Everything becomes a chain reaction, which is why it is important for us to work collaboratively. None of our problems are in isolation—even if they appear to be. We have to work with developmental education and provide sufficient bridges to get our students to an acceptable academic level.

Do we have enough classes? Do we have enough sections to bridge the many need levels? Is it enough to say to a student, "You need developmental math. Come back in two years when there is a section open that you can take, and in the meantime, go ahead and take whatever you want"? In fact, that is what some colleges are forced to say simply because they do not have in place what is needed for remedial students.

This situation is due to limited resources and limited facilities. We are presently struggling at my institution with the balance between developmental education course offerings and university transfer-level courses. Curriculum balance is a complicated issue.

When we examine the modeling of team effectiveness, we must identify a specific issue. Based on that identification, we can develop goals, roles, procedures, and relationships. Who is going to do what, when, where? Who is accountable and who will be held responsible? These are short-term collaborative efforts that bring us together.

I have found that task forces work much better than committees for such efforts because people prefer the timeliness of problem resolution. In terms of an effective initial exercise using collaboration, I would recommend task forces for the examination of issues. There is no need to allow collaborative efforts to get bogged down by a committee. This does not devalue the work of college committees. Standing committees are important for addressing continuing issues, but task forces work effectively for collaborative efforts.

Some community college issues that are appropriate for collaboration within the institution are staff development, literacy, economic development, international education, and evening support services. Evening students pay the same tuition and fees on most community college campuses as day students, and yet the amount of support services provided for those students may not be equitable. That is a real issue for cross-campus deliberation.

Another critical area for collaboration is workplace educational opportunity— the offering of noncredit and credit courses for employees of local businesses. We need to present a joint effort when we approach business and industry. This is a good area for internal collaboration. We need to respond to business and industry needs by combining our college resources to deliver the service.

We have wonderful opportunities for collaboration in community colleges. These opportunities present great challenges. We have seized our opportunities and accomplished many things because we have a lot of good people. We have a lot of talented people. Why not make sure that we forge ahead using all of our collective talents, rather than having any one individual take the lead? There is much for us to do to meet the challenges ahead. Our success will be measured mostly by what we do together, not by what any of us has done alone.

Jerry Sue Owens is president of Lakewood Community College, White Bear Lake, Minnesota.

CHAPTER NINE

The Planning-Development Link

By Paul C. Gianini, Jr. and Wm. Michael Hooks

A S THE UNITED STATES begins the final decade of the twentieth century, it finds itself in the midst of a profound restructuring with major economic, demographic, political, technological, and environmental changes occurring. The restructuring process is expected to move even faster during the 1990s than in previous decades. These forces will place greater pressure on community colleges as they struggle with complex issues such as limited funding, increasing diversity of the student population, technological innovations, accountability pressures, and competition for students. At the same time, our institutions must seek to improve services to students by providing faculty and staff with the resources to continue to be innovative and effective.

Institutions need to strategically position themselves to acquire the necessary resources to maintain their development and renewal process. The steps that an institution must fulfill to attain its vision and mission statement can only be achieved with sufficient human and fiscal resources.

An approach being used by some community colleges today involves establishing a comprehensive planning process and linking it to resource development. A comprehensive planning process enables institutions to determine needs and problems and to establish strategic directions and priorities. On the other hand, external forces, if allowed to, can work against collegewide initiatives such as planning and resource development by creating a mind-set that results in a fragmented fire-fighting approach to operations. Comprehensive planning creates a different mind-set that promotes the involvement of faculty and staff not only in the planning process, but also in the implementation and evaluation of short-term and long-term goals and objectives.

A major reason why many colleges have become involved in comprehensive planning is simply due to lack of resources and the need to focus the energies of the institution. Involving the full spectrum of faculty and staff in the process permits the integration of their plans into a larger set of institutional priorities. The planning process develops leadership and a desire to achieve academic excellence.

Planning and Resource Development

In many institutions, resource development staff are looking externally for funding sources and trying to establish a match with internal needs. Traditionally, the development office writes a complete proposal or handles only the final preparation. Regardless of the approach used, an individual or a team of people, sometimes with assistance from external consultants, must be able to develop a suitable proposal. The process must include the establishment of a plan and the preparation of the grant submission document.

There are several disadvantages to this approach. First, considerable time and energy must be expended by the resource development office not only in preparing the grant proposal, but also in developing or working with others in the development of the plan itself. Second, there might be a tendency to try to create a plan that is inconsistent with the mission and goals of the institution in an effort to be successful in securing external funding. Without realizing all of the consequences, an institution may find itself moving in too many different, and possibly incompatible, directions at once. Third, the random development of proposals may result in projects being developed that are inconsistent with one another and stretch the resources of the institution. Fourth, the effort required to develop a $2,000 proposal may be just as time-consuming as that needed to develop a $200,000 proposal, which has a more substantial impact upon the institution.

The clear alternative to the traditional role of resource development is to link the comprehensive planning process with resource development. A comprehensive planning approach provides a way to monitor a rapidly changing environment, identify preferred alternative futures, and select the best strategies to ensure continuing growth, development, renewal, and survival. By linking comprehensive planning and resource development, a reciprocal synergistic relationship is created.

An integrated planning, management, and evaluation model provides a way to guide an institution through the comprehensive planning process. The model is composed of five stages: preplanning, strategic planning, operational planning, management, and evaluation.

Even though a formal plan may not have been developed previously, every institution will have information regarding various components of a planning, management, and evaluation system already in operation. Documents in various formats (i.e., memorandums, reports, concept papers, and proposals) typically are located in various offices within the institution. Comprehensive plans must be specific to a given institution and developed through broad-based involvement of faculty and staff. An institution cannot simply replicate the exact process at another institution. The model for development of a comprehensive plan must be modified to fit the unique characteristics and traditions of each institution and must be allowed to evolve over time as refinements and changes are made based on both internal and external conditions.

First, the preplanning stage involves the establishment of planning resources (staff, facilities, and equipment), determination of planning techniques (information and software), and the development of planning strategies. These strategies should include a timetable, an assignment of responsibilities, and a description of the process.

Second, the strategic planning stage provides a broad-based, long-range perspective for comprehensive planning. An important initial activity involves the determination of the institution's overall purpose and direction. The review of the mission provides a strong foundation for the planning process. Most colleges have vision, values, and mission statements that document their beliefs, potential future, fundamental purposes, and long-range aspirations. The values statement reflects those beliefs and strong preferences that are used to guide the institution in the development of its vision, mission, goals, and operational procedures.

Published values may differ from those that are really practiced within the institution. The values statement should reflect the important principles that are believed in and actually practiced at the institution. The vision statement provides a reason for being and a compelling picture of a preferred future of the college. The vision frequently is a short statement provided by the chief executive officer, intended to capture the imagination of the faculty and staff and instill a level of confidence that the institution has a certain degree of control over its destiny. An example of this type of statement is found in the Midlands Technical College, South Carolina, planning document, *Vision for Excellence*.

A broad statement of the fundamental purposes of the institution should be captured in the mission statement, which should provide a philosophical, value-oriented declaration of purpose as well as a description of the role and scope of the institution. The mission should reflect affiliation, constituencies, and markets. The institution's role describes what it does and differentiates it from other colleges in terms of level and range of programs.

One way to evaluate the quality of the mission statement is in terms of its uniqueness to a specific institution. Many mission statements are so general that they could not be differentiated from those of other institutions. In such cases, the name of the college could easily be switched and nobody would know the difference. The uniqueness of the institution should be identified in such a way that individuals, both internally and externally, know that these statements refer to a particular institution. The combined effect of these statements should present an image of the institution that is dynamic, integrated, and worth doing.

A second activity in the strategic planning stage is to determine needs, problems, and deficiencies. Information needs to be collected from internal and external environments. In assessing the external environment, one must selectively look for trends, issues, and projections that are or could impact the institution. Trends are changes that are currently underway based upon the analysis of both quantitative and qualitative data. Relevant data can be collected regarding local, state, regional, national, and global trends in a number of categories, including demographic, economic, political, technological, educational, and environmental. These data should be examined by institutions for both threats and opportunities.

Trend data can be identified not only from newspapers, magazines, and journals, but also by working with other institutions at the local level. For example, planners from public schools, higher education institutions, and other appropriate agencies might meet periodically to document and share trends and incorporate them into reports for both planning and public information purposes. Once trends are identified, issues can be analyzed and projections can be developed.

Strategic issues refer to emerging and current forces that may have an impact upon the college. Issues should be linked directly to the strategic directions of the institution. Some colleges have identified a group of strategic issues that are expected to have the greatest effect on the institution and assigned people to track developments in those areas and make periodic progress reports to the president and other college decision makers.

One advantage of distributing responsibility for the development of one- to two-page briefing papers is to develop expertise and leadership among decision makers. Those individuals assigned to track specific issues provide alternative approaches to dealing with the issues and make recommendations. Thus, discussions can be held on how the college will handle each issue from a public relations, legal, academic, and financial standpoint.

The assessment of internal strengths and weaknesses at an institution can be built around program, personnel, and student data. Increasing numbers of institutions are creating annual fact books or statistical histories, which provide enrollment, financial aid, high school, assessment, demographic, graduate, personnel, and other data. To be most effective for analysis purposes, these data should reflect trends over time. Increasing numbers of institutions are placing greater emphasis on longitudinal student tracking systems, monitoring student cohorts in terms of progress, retention, outcomes, and performance of graduates on standardized exams, at four-year institutions, and in their careers.

Both internal and external factors should be used to focus on the identification of needs, problems, and deficiencies that are student-related. A frequent error made by institutions is to overlook the needs and problems of students and to go immediately to possible solutions. The problem is not whether or not the college needs more computer equipment, software, labs, and special programs; the underlying problem is that students may not have access to the appropriate programs, resources, and services to enable them to be competitive and successful in today's rapidly changing, competitive society.

Different strategies can be used to determine problems and deficiencies, to develop assumptions and conclusions, and to specify strategic directions for the institution, including focus groups, planning committees, and collegewide meetings. The result of this process should be a set of broad-based, long-range goals that can be used as umbrella statements under which more specific goals and objectives can be grouped. Frequently these goals include statements about teaching excellence, quality staff, student services, marketing strategies, funding initiatives, community and economic development, and information systems (see Figure 1).

Figure 1. Valencia Community College Long-Range Goals 1990–91—1994–95

Goal 1. Continue to pursue excellence in education to the limit of the college's fiscal and human resources.

Goal 2. Provide for the recruitment, professional renewal, and maintenance of quality staff who support holistic learning.

Goal 3. Establish coordinated student services programs that support the students' total educational experience, increase the student success rate, and manage enrollment.

Goal 4. Increase funding sources to assist the college in strengthening the quality of programs and services.

Goal 5. Strengthen relationships through increased communication and articulation between Valencia Community College and area schools, vocational/technical centers, and four-year colleges and universities to enhance access and retention.

Goal 6. Establish management procedures and an integrated management information system that enhances decision making and increases the effectiveness of the college in utilizing its resources to improve academic quality and student success.

Goal 7. Develop and implement a comprehensive local, state, and national marketing program that will inform specific constituencies and the community of the college's academic quality, support services, and diversity of programs.

Goal 8. Establish partnerships with local business, industry, and government that support and stimulate the economic development of the community.

A number of institutions have also established statements of expected student outcomes that reflect competencies that students should achieve by the time they complete particular degree programs (see Figure 2). Both empirical and theoretical models are being used. Student outcomes provide a method for identifying student-based problems and deficiencies that can be linked directly to institutional problems and deficiencies.

In the third stage, operational planning, faculty and staff involvement is especially important. This stage provides a framework that integrates strategic goals with student outcomes for the identification of measurable objectives, implementation strategies, and an evaluation plan. While objectives may be either process- or product-oriented, emphasis should be given to measurable results over a specific time period. Within each objective, specific tasks can be delineated. Resource requirements must be identified, and performance evaluation measures specified.

Figure 2. Educational Outcomes: Competencies of a Valencia Graduate

> 1. Think critically and make reasoned choices by acquiring, analyzing, synthesizing, and evaluating knowledge.
> 2. Read, listen, write, and speak effectively.
> 3. Understand and use quantitative information.
> 4. Clarify personal strengths, values, and goals in relation to cultural values.
> 5. Have the knowledge and skills necessary for effective citizenship.
> 6. Recognize the value of aesthetics.
> 7. Recognize the value of physical and mental health.

The evaluation plan should include three major components: student performance; unit/program performance; and employee performance. Measurements of student performance should include formative assessments at the course, department, and program level as students move through the institution, as well as post-program gauges of success such as standardized exams upon exit from the institution, continuation in upper-division programs, and success in chosen occupations.

Typically, program/unit reviews are conducted only in vocational and technical programs, but they should be completed, at a minimum, every five years at the division, program, and department level for all instructional programs as well as administrative areas.

Performance evaluations of all faculty and staff are typically conducted on an annual or biannual basis. Employee actions that are linked to the institutional goals and student outcomes should be included in these assessments. All three types of evaluation—student performance, unit/program performance, and faculty and staff performance—should specify how the results will be used to make improvements and document the improvements made.

The fourth stage of planning, the management phase, requires the assignment of responsibility and the allocation of resources. The implementation of management procedures is coordinated by the administrative staff who will document the actual results.

Last, the evaluation stage refers to those procedures used to compare the plan with actual outcomes and implement changes and improvements. Evaluation procedures should include both analysis and synthesis of a variety of data in determining an institution's overall effectiveness.

The purpose of the planning management and evaluation model is to determine an institution's effectiveness over the short, intermediate, and long range. The short-range focus is on efficiency, productivity, and satisfaction; the intermediate-range is on development and innovation; and the long-range focus is on survival, renewal, reaffirmation of accreditation, and self-actualization. The comprehensive planning process results in a strong foundation, which enables an institution to identify strategic directions, operational procedures, and assessment measures.

The Role of Resource Development

Resource development plays a significant role in making an institution's comprehensive planning process work effectively. Conversely, the comprehensive planning process is a major factor in determining an institution's success at resource development. The two processes enable each other, and both support the development of faculty and staff leadership capacities.

Comprehensive planning can serve as the single most important activity impacting resource development. As those familiar with proposals are aware, a grant is basically a plan expressed with a narrative describing needs, goals, objectives, and implementation strategies along with a budget format. The comprehensive plan serves as a source of ideas for grants. All grants are rooted in the plan and can be viewed as pieces of the strategic plan.

Viewed from this angle, comprehensive planning processes focus and direct the resource development process and allow an institution to be proactive in seeking funds for internally developed ideas rather than reacting to whatever agendas funding agencies may have established. Further, they provide a framework of priorities within which the college can make wise choices about the use of resource development time.

Looking at the linkage between comprehensive planning and resource development from another angle, success at resource development provides a positive setting in which comprehensive planning can occur. Resource development can create this positive impact if faculty and staff believe in the resource development capability and enjoy their involvement. If faculty actually believe that their efforts will result in funding that can be used to provide better programs and services to their students, they will be willing to dream larger dreams and to share those dreams. In addition, they will not create barriers that result in the censorship of their ideas in the mistaken belief that the college could never find the resources to implement them. A successful resource development capacity eliminates the barriers that create an artificial limit on an institution's planning process.

For resource development to take full advantage of a comprehensive planning process, the institution must develop a philosophy that differs significantly from that in place at other community colleges, a philosophy that supports the involvement of faculty and staff, using their talents and resources in the most effective and efficient way. The organizational climate must encourage innovative thinking, value-positive change, and risk taking. External funding is needed to test ideas and to provide seed money to launch new programs and expand existing programs. In most cases, the plan should include steps that will result in activities that can become self-supporting after the grant ends rather than drain institutional resources.

Colleges must strive to be proactive. Various collaborative teams should develop the college plan and then seek existing funding programs or attempt to create new funding opportunities that will support the plan. In every real sense, colleges should react to grant opportunities by creating their own opportunities through linking planning and development.

According to Susan Kelley, president of the Florida Council for Resource Development, an institution's plan helps strengthen its resource development efforts and nurtures its vision in five ways:

• The plan sets a standard of excellence for the entire institution. Ideas that are put forward must aspire to that standard, or they will not find their way into the plan.

• The plan helps the college staff see how single, seemingly isolated activities contribute to the college's total effort.

• The plan frees faculty and staff to dream and to structure those dreams into workable programs with plans that help them to be achieved. While the plan imparts a long-term vision, it also requires us to be disciplined enough to consider the implications of all of our actions both today and tomorrow. Planning enables us to transcend the present situation.

• The planning process with its emphasis on resource development is a significant morale booster. It enables faculty and staff to see a congruence between personal and institutional goals. It enables faculty and staff to take ownership of the proposed grant-funded activity and motivate them throughout its creation and implementation.

• Planning plays a control function, helping the college to identify deviations from the norm, not to squash innovation, but to the contrary, to identify new trends and ideas, to point out gaps in what we are doing. The planning process helps us to identify legitimate differences and accommodate diversity.

Planning and resource development are a testament to shared leadership. They are not characteristics of individuals. They are the product of teams of leaders who draw upon the skills of many members. Planning and resource development processes work in measurable, interrelated ways because more than one person is committed to making them work, more than one person's performance is measured in terms of how well they work, and more than one person is provided with the opportunity to lead. The team approach encourages everyone in the planning and resource development process to be a star in his or her own right, while shining ever more brightly when viewed as one of the many stars that make up the college team.

Paul C. Gianini, Jr. is president and Wm. Michael Hooks is vice president for planning, research, and development at Valencia Community College, Orlando, Florida.

CHAPTER TEN

A Statewide Perspective

By Ronald J. Horvath

T HE OTHER CONTRIBUTORS to this book have revealed many of the imperatives that our institutions must successfully address in the decade ahead. While some pertain to a small number of institutions, most are issues that confront us all. Some will be planned for by individual institutions, while others will require a greater level of public policy support.

The state of Kentucky recently set out on a focused process of examining the twenty-five-year history of the Kentucky Community College System by a thirty-five-member independent commission, three-fourths of whom were non-educators. This state-level planning process is illustrative of how state policy makers can, through planning, change the course of our institutions.

This chapter will examine the dynamics and benefits of the statewide planning process through the perspective of *more, better, fewer, and less*.

Return with me to those thrilling days of yesteryear when our hormones flowed freely, our cholesterol was low, and we studied Civics 101 in junior high school or middle school. Our civics teachers instilled in us the concept that governments exist to serve the people. We further learned that we elect people to carry out our mandates. Simply stated, this is democracy in action.

What we didn't fully appreciate in junior high is that the goal of serving one's constituents is a complex process, mired in election campaigns. But this too is a part of the democratic process, which ultimately produces—in a broad general sense—the will of the people.

Candidates for elected offices have one common goal—to get elected. Incumbents who stand for re-election also have one common goal—to get re-elected. All else becomes secondary to the process that we Americans label the democratic way. Voters, in turn, respond positively or negatively to candidates and to their campaign messages. We elect those whose overall pledges, personalities, and priorities closely match our own, and we expect those people to carry out our agenda for the future.

What many voters fail to realize, of course, is that elected officials are not the ones who develop long-range plans to serve the people of a particular state or commonwealth. Almost without exception that task falls to the various state agencies created for a particular purpose. Occasionally, however, that planning function can include groups external to these agencies.

In a very simplistic way, the overall priorities and goals of politicians and agencies revolve around four simple words: more, better, fewer, and less. The people want more jobs, more services, more and better health care, more roads, better schools, more laws, more happiness, fewer drop-outs, fewer welfare recipients, less taxes, and less unemployment.

Very few people think of candidates, campaigns, elections, or planning as rooted in these four simple words. And yet, is it totally unrealistic to think of these processes in terms of more, better, fewer, and less?

Let me restate my initial premise—candidates for elected office identify issues and develop priorities to address those issues. Many voters are unaware of the various party platforms that are developed with some acrimony and debate prior to an election campaign. Nevertheless, these platforms focus on the candidates's priorities and more often than not become the nucleus of long-range planning efforts that usually fall to government agencies.

About the only time that these platform planks are evaluated is at re-election time, when the incumbent defends and the challenger attacks. New platforms are written or old ones are revised. And thus, the process of setting priorities—more, better, fewer, and less—begins anew.

Agencies are usually evaluated by their ability to react to new or modified priorities as they continue the planning process and the development of operational strategies. Agency leaders, department heads, and program planners come and go as soon as elections are settled and the voters have spoken. But the process of planning goes on because the carry-over employees, the lifeblood of any agency or institution, perform their functions and carry out the new priorities of more, better, fewer, and less. The everyday process of agency planning, as complex as it might be, does produce common goals, timetables, and consensus. Therein lies its value—order is maintained and chaos averted.

But planning for its own sake is a plague. Millions upon millions of pages of detailed plans have been written, shredded, and dumped. Beautifully bound documents line the shelves of every agency and institution in this country. We groan under the weight of our own creations, and, if we are not careful, they will bury us. Elaborate planning systems developed by well-meaning bureaucrats tend to take on a life of their own.

Prior to his appointment as president of the World Bank in 1968, Robert McNamara rose to political prominence as Secretary of Defense in the Kennedy and Johnson administrations. Secretary McNamara had gained national attention as president of Ford Motor Company, where he developed the Planning, Programming, and Budgeting System (PPBS). Appointed to the high-level cabinet position, McNamara imposed a highly centralized budget and allocation system on a federal agency that was already clogged by bureaucratic planners. PPBS was a marvelous paperwork exercise that produced nothing but more paperwork.

To make matters worse, PPBS filtered down in modified form to some state governments. As a young administrator at a community college in Pennsylvania in the late 1960s, I became one of the victims of PPBS, which was based on functions and missions. I can still recall painfully the countless hours that all of us at the college spent filling out elaborate and lengthy forms that ultimately resulted in a grandiose 200-page document for the college. The end result was nothing but an exercise in elaborate planning, number crunching, duplicating, stapling, filing, and finally shelving! Perhaps that is one reason why I favor the simplistic planning priorities of more, better, fewer, and less.

Underlying these priorities, as well as the action plans developed to implement them, is a philosophy or a set of values or beliefs. These values, which should be stated succinctly and committed to paper, can and do play a vital role in the planning process of an institution—be it an agency of government, a philanthropic association, a community college, or an independent commission. What we believe about ourselves, our institutions, and our roles within the context of a larger society forms the nucleus of what we plan and how we react.

Three simple value statements within the Statement of Institutional Values developed at Jefferson Community College sum up our stated role as an institution of higher education within a system of community colleges: "We hold this college in trust for the people of Kentucky. . . The college exists to enable students to earn a college education . . . All college personnel must contribute to and be supportive of the educational mission of the college."

As administrators, faculty, and staff members, we acknowledge that the college does not belong to us, nor does it exist to serve us. Quite to the contrary, we are the guardians of the college and thus have an obligation to maintain it, to improve it, to nurture it, and to monitor its progress. Should we fail or should we falter in these ultimate challenges, then we, or some other entity with the legal authority to do so, should padlock its doors.

Considering the alternatives, it certainly does behoove us to pause and reflect on whether we are in step with the priorities of the various systems and subsystems within which we operate and function.

There is one other method not frequently used to achieve similar results without the constraints of self-serving or vested interests. Specifically, an alternative is to use the expertise of groups not affiliated with a state agency or any other arm of government. What started out as a focused process of examining the history of the Kentucky Community College System by an independent commission ultimately evolved into a set of priorities and strategic activities for the future. These priorities, in turn, evolved into a unified sense of purpose for the fourteen community colleges located around the Commonwealth of Kentucky.

There were three remarkable dimensions of this process: 75 percent (twenty-six out of thirty-five) of Community College Futures Commission members were non-educators; the final document, *Community Colleges: Pathway to Kentucky's Future*, was only thirty pages long and the executive summary only four pages; and the report presented both a forward and a backward look at the community college system.

In response to the challenges released in the AACJC Futures Commission report, *Building Communities,* the chancellor for the Kentucky Community College System set into motion in late spring 1988 a plan to examine the achievements of the system's two-year colleges.

A former Kentucky governor, under whose executive leadership the community college system was established in 1962, accepted the chancellor's offer to co-chair the commission, to which thirty-four other prominent Kentucky residents were named.

Seven major topics were identified as the basic elements for the Kentucky Commission's review: mission; access; college and community partnerships; economic development; institutional effectiveness; governance; and resources. Four major meetings of two to three days each were scheduled during the 1988–89 academic year to address the seven topics. A final forum was held in September 1989 to release the commission's report as a part of the system's twenty-fifth anniversary celebration. The main speaker for the gala event was the current Kentucky governor, who is a staunch community college advocate. This September meeting preceded the General Assembly's 1990 legislative session by four months.

The format for the four major commission meetings included background and information papers sent to the members prior to each meeting, guest speakers to add regional and national perspectives, small group discussions, consensus building, recommendations for the future, a detailed rationale for each recommendation, priority setting, and suggested strategic activities.

One example of the commission's focus and its findings was access. The following question was thoroughly examined: "Should the open admission concept be continued?" Ultimately, the commission strongly supported open admissions as the realistic access point for the majority of people who desired to pursue a college education. But rather than simply endorsing the concept, the commission tied open admissions to the quality of life, to economic accessibility, and to economically disadvantaged citizens. The commission stated succinctly, "Higher education should be inclusive rather than exclusive."

Several other key ideas that evolved during the deliberations of access are worth citing:

"Community colleges across the nation, and especially in Kentucky, are dedicated to empowering people through knowledge. Kentucky's citizens from all walks of life . . . have responded to the system's open-door policy."

"Many personal paths are blocked by barriers such as poverty, age, race, or other constraints. The Community College System is committed to removing those barriers."

"Our state's need for educated and trained workers is so great that we cannot hope to meet the challenge without escalating our current approaches through extended campuses."

These powerful, powerful words are both an endorsement and a challenge. But the commission did not stop with a simple endorsement of access. The members developed eight strategies to solidify and expand the goal of open access:

• Formulate agreements and alliances with external agencies for the purpose of sharing instructional resources and facilities that can increase access to courses and services

• Institute special activities to recruit, retain, and graduate minority students

• Plan for the creation of new community colleges and off-campus sites and centers in areas where the population justifies expansion

• Use telecommunications to expand access to community college programs

• Launch a marketing campaign that highlights access to community college programs and activities

• Support and promote the use of technology as a tool for teaching and learning

• Provide incentives to students to move from the completion of the GED to earning an associate degree

• Offer more programs in partnerships with high schools

These are dynamite words from a group of lay citizens who had no vested interest in the colleges other than to insure that these educational services to the citizens continued and expanded.

In the letter included in the commission's final report, the commission chairman offered these words:

Our hope is that the executive and legislative leaders understand that the community college system is one of the primary vehicles by which our state can gain an image of excellence and economic strength, both desperately needed in Kentucky. Our broadest recommendation to the executive and legislative branches of government is to encourage those in charge of the system to "forge ahead" and make the system the best in the nation. The potential is there!

The current governor endorsed the report, pledged to increase the funding for community colleges, and delivered on that promise. In addition, the Kentucky Council on Higher Education revised its funding formula to guarantee a more equitable distribution of resources for the community colleges both now and in the future.

These outcomes certainly underscore the success of this "non-agency" approach to planning. But the overwhelmingly positive Futures Commission report was merely the catalyst that brought not only recognition to the work of the community colleges, but also a future focus to that work. The commission members insisted that a follow-up report on the colleges' activities be developed during the 1989–90 academic year and that the commission be reconvened in November 1990 to assess, once again, the effectiveness of the colleges, the impact of their report, the executive and legislative responses to their recommendations, and the status of the community colleges.

Thus, when the commission's report was formally released to the public in fall 1989, the real work for the fourteen system colleges began in earnest. Each college was required to submit an interim report in January 1990 detailing its activities *vis à vis* the commission's recommendations. The interim report for the entire system exceeded 750 pages. The final report was developed into a comprehensive document presented to the commission at its follow-up meeting.

Furthermore, several individual colleges tied their 1990–91 budget requests to specific recommendations contained in the report.

What better way to justify requests for more, better, fewer, and less than to link them with the priorities of prominent community leaders from all walks of life. With the increased funding provided by the governor and the General Assembly and with college budget requests linked to the commission's priorities and strategic activities, the Kentucky Community College System has been rejuvenated and revitalized.

Ronald J. Horvath is president of Jefferson Community College, Louisville, Kentucky.

PART TWO

THE
ISSUES

CHAPTER ELEVEN

National Issues, Local Action

By David Viar

TODAY OUR NATION is facing very serious problems that will affect each one of us if they are not addressed in the near future. You cannot possibly plan for the future if you do not know where you are today, and the reality of today does not point to a promising future.

The national problems are being talked about and written about. They are, on occasion, being debated in political campaigns and in the halls of Congress. But national solutions do not appear to be on the horizon. The solutions are ultimately going to come at the community level, and that is why institutional planning for community colleges is so very important.

The national problems about which I write are ones that fit our business—the business of serving the education needs of the citizens of our communities. People: That is really what we are all about. Therefore, as we look at these national policy issues, let us look at them as people issues.

According to Marian Wright Edelman of the Children's Defense Fund, one in four pre-schoolers is poor. For Blacks it is one in two. One in six has no health insurance. One in two has a mother in the work force and is not getting adequate child care. One in five is going to be a pre-teen parent. One in seven is going to drop out of school. Edelman says we lose about 10,000 children every year to poverty. This is a recipe for national disaster. These children are the work force of the year 2000, and in planning for the future you have to think about them.

A report from the National Institutes of Medicines's National Forum on the Future of Children and Family says that we need to prepare our young for entry into the labor force and to become productive members of society. Yet there is a concern about the ability of our social and educational institutions to react and respond to the problems and issues. Are you prepared to respond, to react, to deal with those issues?

It is estimated that one-third of the homeless today are families with children, and this segment is growing rapidly. Too often when we talk about the homeless problem, we don't even think about that aspect. These homeless children have very little chance for an education.

As the homeless numbers grow, studies are showing that illiteracy is a key reason for much of that homelessness. A sampling of the homeless taken by the Volunteers of America of Greater New York shows that 60 percent read below the fifth-grade level.

The figures for high school drop-outs are startling. Seven hundred thousand students drop out of high school each year. The average high school drop-out rate across the country is 26 percent, but in many areas it is as high as 40 percent. Twenty million young people are not college-bound. Fifty percent of those who are leaving high school do not intend to go on to get a baccalaureate degree or to participate in a postsecondary education program.

There is a large untapped resource out there, and it is untapped not because we need students, but because these are people who must be served in our educational programs if our society is to move forward.

According to some studies, 23 million people in the United States are functionally illiterate. We can debate as educators the definition of "functionally illiterate," and we can question the numbers. But even if the actual number is a fraction of that 23 million, it is far too high. The Southport Institute for Policy Analysis's report on adult literacy points out that in spite of the huge numbers, only three to four million people right now are being reached in literacy programs, and that is with an average annual expenditure of just $200 per individual as compared to a nationwide average of $4,000 per year for our K-12 students.

Medical research shows that retirees who stay active and keep learning are healthier. By the year 2000 there will be over thirty-five million people over sixty-five, and it is going to be very important to look closely at what we are doing in our colleges and across the country to address the needs of those individuals. As a report from the Congress on Aging stated, "Times change, and it is now the older population and those close to them whose educational needs are not being met."

Harvard economist Lester Thurow, citing Bureau of the Census and Federal Reserve Board data, says, "The rich are getting richer, the poor are increasing in number, and the middle class has trouble holding its own. We are seeing a surge toward inequality." This leads to a major problem that we face in our country, and that is significant labor shortages.

The people problems cited here are growing and growing, compounded by other problems such as crime and drugs. Unfortunately, these problems, almost all of which relate to education, are coming at the very time we are faced with the requirements of a new service economy. We need workers with new skills to compete in a world market, and we are not finding those people.

As reported in a study commissioned by the U.S. Department of Labor, *Workforce 2000*, between now and the year 2000 a majority of all new jobs created will require some postsecondary education. One-third of all jobs will require college graduates. Right now that figure is only about 20 percent. Even if we go beyond the technical skills jobs, the least-skilled jobs will require a command of reading, computing, and thinking that was once necessary only for professionals.

Minorities, women, and immigrants are going to comprise five-sixths of the net additions to the work force, yet our country has a poor track record of serving these groups the kind of education and skill training they desperately need.

We face the challenge in this country of upgrading by 45 percent the skills of twenty-five million American workers by the year 2000 if we are to remain competitive.

As *Workforce 2000* concludes, "Promoting world growth, boosting the service industry productivity, stimulating a more flexible work force, providing for the needs of working families with children, bringing minorities into the work force, and improving the educational preparation of workers are among the most important, pressing items on the nation's agenda." These are issues that will not go away by themselves. The time to address them is now, and we must consider these as we deal with planning our institutions' future directions.

Are these national problems also problems elsewhere? As institutions plan they must address this question. As you consider local data, do not forget how interconnected we are in this country. Even if you do not find that these problems now exist in your community and are not yet directly visible to you, indirectly throughout the country, in each area, in each region, we will begin to feel an economic ripple building to a tidal wave of economic disaster if change does not occur.

Arthur Levine, president of Bradford College, says, "We are now living through a period of the most profound demographic, economic, social, and technological change since the Industrial Revolution. When societies change dramatically as they periodically do, their social and educational institutions, hard-pressed to keep pace, can take years to readjust to new conditions."

We do not have time for years of readjustment. We cannot take the time. Throughout our brief history we in the community colleges have been proud of being flexible and of being able to meet change. Now is our time to prove it. Whether it is a community college in California, Michigan, Texas, or New Jersey, we have to deal with the people issues. We must prove that we can be flexible and change to meet those needs.

How can community colleges respond to national policy? That question presupposes that there is a national policy. Unfortunately, I do not see that there is, in fact, a national policy for anyone in the nation's community, junior, and technical colleges to implement. There is no cohesive, coordinated national policy to address people issues.

Over the years, there have been significant federal education initiatives. The Perkins Vocational Technical Education Act, Pell Grants, Stafford Loans, and the Adult Education Act provide funds to community colleges and our students. The McKinney Act, which dealt with the homeless situation, included several million dollars to be distributed among the states for dealing with the literacy problem among the homeless. The Job Training Partnership Act was certainly a major federal effort to assist people who needed training.

The welfare reform passed last year had a major provision requiring states to have training and education programs in place.

There is some effort to address our people issues, but all of these are, at best, Band-Aid approaches. At their finest they are, in the terms of a recent report on adult literacy, excellent jump-start solutions to get us stirred up. They are not going to solve the problems. They are ways of identifying problems and getting the state and local governments to begin to deal with them. And even if there was in Congress a major recognition of these problems and a willingness to step forward and deal with them, with the growing federal budget deficit there is little money to help in these kinds of programs.

So, it is important to recognize that ultimately the solutions to these national policy problems rest in the community. David Matthews, president of the Kettering Foundation, says, "We must take a grass-roots approach to solving our problems. Citizens must create their own purpose, build common ground, generate political will, and transform private individuals into public citizens. We must be about building community."

In fact, that was the theme taken by AACJC's Commission on the Future of Community Colleges. We must be about building community. The solutions are in our local communities and in our local colleges.

As these issues are addressed, the demands placed on our institutions include the increased developmental education needs of the returning adult learner and the ill-prepared, ill-equipped student coming directly out of high school; the issue of adult literacy; the question of minority access, recruitment, and retention; the need to increase the rate of participation in postsecondary education; the changing educational needs of the work force; and all the expenses that are related to developing the necessary curricula and supplying the needed instructional equipment to meet the ever-demanding, ever-changing technology.

Several years ago, there was a nationwide trend by state legislators and governors to criticize community colleges for wanting to be all things to all people. We found in state after state the development of commissions and study groups to look at the community college mission. Amazingly, to those who began to look at us, and not so amazingly to those who work in and for the community colleges, the conclusion was that the comprehensive mission of the community college was essential.

What state policy makers said in state after state was, "You must maintain your comprehensive education mission and the services you are providing and expand further the quality of the education support services." There are few legislators or governors now saying community colleges should deal only with baccalaureate transfer programs or only technical education. That is past.

There is a big job to do, and those of you who have committed to serve your local communities need to recognize the national policy issues. They are significant, and they are people-related. The solutions lie in our education institutions.

Your response to the national policy vacuum should be to take the lead. Do not wait to respond to national policy directives from the federal government. Those are not going to come. The solutions must be in the community.

As each community, junior, and technical college plans, it must not forget the people. We must set a strong and courageous agenda for action. We must then tell the story with vigor throughout the community and throughout each state. We must be advocates for the education needs of our people . . . because a promising future doesn't just happen.

David Viar is executive director of the Community College League of California, Sacramento, California.

CHAPTER TWELVE

Equality of Opportunity

By Judith Eaton

I F SOMETHING INTERESTING or exciting or problematic or challenging happens in higher education, it likely happens first in a community college. When women started attending higher education institutions in significantly increased numbers, community college enrollments first reflected this change. A similar circumstance occurred with minorities. The tremendous emphasis on career education in higher education first occurred in the community colleges. The problems of underpreparedness we began to experience among students in the late 1960s and into the 1970s were first felt in our nation's community colleges.

In this context of community colleges as the first arena of educational change, there are three major issues I wish to address: the transfer function; majority students (and I do not mean White students); and the management of race in higher education.

When I talk about the transfer function, I am greatly concerned about the capacity within our colleges to build opportunity for educational mobility from community colleges to four-year universities. Generally, when I talk about transfer, people say, "Here she goes, she's going after those students of a suspiciously elite character. She wants special recruitment programs." But that is not my intent.

Transfer is not a program; it is not a curriculum. It is student behavior, or, at the very least, student intent. Transfer, we need to remind ourselves, involves both liberal arts and career education students in community colleges. At my former institution, we had more associate of applied science graduates transferring than we had either associate of general studies, associate of arts, or associate of science graduates transfer. Transfer is an opportunity that we have a tendency to overlook when we deal with both the short- and long-range goals of our students.

Successful transfer is part of our academic legitimacy; it affirms that we are valued by the higher education community. Transfer gives meaning to access. We all know that more than 50 percent of the first-time, credit freshmen in colleges and universities are in community colleges. We all know that 30 percent of the women in higher education are in community colleges, and we all know that half the minorities enrolled in colleges and universities are in community colleges. The transfer function helps to make our commitment to diversity in our institutions even more significant.

Perhaps some of you saw Clifford Adelman's article about a year ago in *Change* magazine where he was looking at an analysis of the 1972 high school graduating class who were also community college attendees. His preliminary findings show that about 20 percent of those people attended a community college and attended a four-year school. They did not obtain degrees. About 11 percent went from a community college without earning an associate degree and obtained a baccalaureate, and only 6 percent attained both the associate degree and the baccalaureate degree.

Why are we not even more effective when it comes to transfer? There are a variety of reasons. Transfer is only part of what we do. We spent many years investing heavily in what we called terminal programs. We have a community service function. We have developmental and remedial education responsibilities. Only some of our students want to transfer. Does it make any sense for us to measure our transfer effectiveness by taking into account those people who have no intention of using our institution that way? Another reason for limited transfer effectiveness that is generally offered is that four-year schools are not especially hospitable to transfer. Sometimes this is pointed out in anger and frustration, but other times there are good reasons why four-year schools do not want transfer students. Those reasons extend to include four-year schools that do not want transfer students from other four-year schools, not just community colleges.

We can do more with transfer, these difficulties notwithstanding. We can declare transfer as institutionally important; we can pay greater attention to transfer; and we can manage for transfer. Transfer calls for a serious education program, whether in the liberal arts or career education, a program that makes meaningful academic demands, that engages and involves students, that produces identifiable student gains, and that reflects institutional thinking in some way about general education.

I could describe a number of transfer programs that would meet those criteria. We all know what would be effective in transfer education in our institutions. The point is to focus on it. The point is to extend and enhance our involvement with it. To say that transfer as a function is important or to pay attention to it is also to say that we are willing to think beyond our colleges for our students' educational well-being. We should be encouraging our students in the use of both the community college and the four-year experience as they attempt to develop and to meet their goals.

Transfer is central to our comprehensive educational responsibility for our students. Community college education is wonderful, but it is not enough. There are some hard economic facts that will affirm this for us. There are many, many examples around us where baccalaureate education does even more for people than associate degree education. It is also important not to be stymied by students' immediate education needs. We can accommodate the person who walks into the college and wants three or four or five courses, is working, and has a range of personal responsibilities—and assist that person in the development of his or her longer-range thinking around transfer and baccalaureate education.

Let me now turn to majority students. A college might confer more than 500 degrees at the end of an academic year, but yet might have in excess of 20,000 students. Those students are telling the college what community college students are telling all of us all over the country: "For most of us, degrees do not structure our education." The majority student is the non-degree, part-time student.

Five million students attend community colleges each year; we award approximately 400,000 degrees per year. My point is a straightforward one: The approach in our institutions to program structure needs modification. Let us keep the degrees. They have a good deal of value. But let us also make greater use of other program structures. There is something in between isolated course taking and a degree program. We can talk about "program" in a different sense from degree program. It can be fewer credits. We need some alternative ways, short of the degree, to organize, structure, and inform the educational experience of our students.

The most at-risk student is the isolated course taker. The man or woman who wanders in and about taking a course is least likely to persist, is likely to have a lower GPA than other people in the institution, is less likely to graduate, and is less likely to transfer. Looking at structuring the educational experience short of degrees allows us to do several important things. It allows us, for example, to address the issue of general education, which I think is incredibly difficult to grapple with short of a degree.

Programs short of a degree are important for non-degree transfer students. Many students choose to transfer before getting a degree. Do you want to sanction this behavior as an institution? Do you want to assist these students through the structuring of their education experience? Or, do you want to attempt to keep them until they complete a degree? Programs short of a degree orientation are also vehicles that we can use creatively in our organizations to connect developmental and college-level programs. We can use them for a bridging kind of activity.

Finally, I'd like to address the management of race. Specifically I want to briefly speak to two issues: our hope for equity in society; and academic standards. When I was president of the Community College of Philadelphia, I had a phone call from someone in the community who was concerned about a student. He told me that the student could not get into the college. We are an open-admission institution with millions of dollars in financial aid. I did not understand, and I said, "I'll check into it."

I did check. The student had attended the institution about a year ago. She had applied for financial aid; she did not get it. I asked some questions of some administrators: "What do you mean, she didn't get it? Didn't we help her? Did we behave like a typical bureaucracy? Did we fail to be sensitive and caring?" I found out that we had done a lot of work with the student; we fully assisted her with her financial aid application, provided her with counseling, and assisted her registration efforts. She had not, in the final analysis, brought in the needed papers for processing.

In addition to the federal financial aid at the college, we also have a million-dollar revolving student loan fund. If you are a financial aid student and you register before classes start but too late for financial aid processing, which means that we cannot process your financial aid papers in time for the beginning of the term, then we provide you with some money to get started for the term.

We gave the young woman in question a Community College of Philadelphia loan and helped her (once again) with her financial aid. We expected that she would pay the college back. When she received her aid check, she registered for four classes. She finished the semester. She flunked two of the classes, obtained a D in another one, and received a mark we call "Making Progress" in the fourth class (this means you did not do everything we expected you to do in class but we are going to give you more time to do it).

The student wanted to come back to school. She was on academic probation. We could let her back in for six credits in spite of the academic problems. But she had not paid on the previous semester. Unless she either paid us or made some provision for payment, we could not allow her to register for the next semester. We told her we would help her with her financial aid once again, and that we would work out a payment plan with her, but we had to have some financial commitment from her or we could not register her for classes. This was a long-standing institutional practice.

She agreed to a payment plan. We processed her financial aid, we found her classes. She was supposed to come in and provide us with some money, and she did not.

We devised yet another payment plan to which she agreed. We said, "Look. You are going to be needing to do some work in the learning laboratory at the college as a result of being on academic probation. We want to provide you with some additional tutoring and academic support work while you are here, and we can provide you with a work-study job for part of that time if you will agree that you'll begin to pay us back for the money you owe us." She agreed. And I was relieved. We appeared to have resolved this. I said to myself, "Maybe something will work out, and she'll get her grades up and continue on in school."

The man who had called me initially called back. He was furious with me about this student. He told me a lot of things about my institution that I did not like to hear and that I thought were not true. And then he proceeded to tell me in some very unpleasant language just what kind of a woman I was, and, most importantly, that I was a White woman and therefore racist.

The message to me was that he was a very prominent person in the community, he was a Black man and—even if the college is satisfied and the student is satisfied—he wanted things done a certain way. It was a very, very distressing conversation. And I asked myself, "What is going on here?" I was trying to piece that together because I believe this is a reasonably stark episode, but it is not an unusual one.

A lot of us in community colleges have spent many, many years predicating our actions on the moral and social imperatives of building an equitable society. Many of us came out of the 1960s with a lot of determination, a lot of caring, and a lot of commitment.

But I see something else happening in this society today. I call this a manipulating of that moral imperative. This occurs when White business owners use minorities as fronts to get federal, state, and local funds for minority-owned businesses. I see it when I see White and minority politicians interested primarily in power, not in social good. This, in my view, is what was going on with this man on the telephone with me.

The point here is a painful one: Majority and minority people need to distinguish between those who are more truly concerned to build a better society and those who are more dedicated to cynically manipulating the system for their own ends. The emergence of this phenomenon helps, in part, to explain the Richmond decision of the Supreme Court. It helps to explain the election of David Duke. I offer these comments in the hope that we can identify what is happening and work together to deal with it.

The last issue I want to address in the context of the management of race is academic standards. We are all familiar with the diminishing of standards in the 1960s. We were willing to do this because we valued individual choice, we valued diversity, and we respected individuality and independence. We succeeded in making standards less important.

We continue to argue today in our colleges about standards. We are concerned about standards and racism as reflected in standardized testing and admissions requirements.

Using the 1960s practice of paying less attention to standards as a means to manage the difficult issue of race is not a viable approach for us. It will harm and it has harmed all of us in this society. There are minority leaders and majority leaders who recognize that the society cannot function without a commitment to minimum standards of quality and effectiveness for all.

The issue here is not to eliminate standards but to sustain them with a commitment that is incredibly sensitive to equity issues. We need some shared agreements about how this society must work. Ignoring standards totally as a solution, I argue, will not work. Further, until we adequately deal with the issue of standards, those of us who are other than White men will invariably be viewed with suspicion.

We in the community colleges have witnessed an expansion of access in America that is unprecedented. But especially in the last five years, we have been taking ourselves to task for educational ineffectiveness. To some extent the country has also been taking us to task. Some people would like to maintain that there is a causal relationship between expanded access and educational ineffectiveness. I do not think this is sustainable, but I think that it is a warning and a challenge, especially to those of us in community colleges. We must be institutions of serious academic purpose if we are going to be vehicles for democratic hope.

Judith Eaton is director of the National Center for Academic Achievement and Transfer and vice president, the American Council on Education in Washington, D.C.

CHAPTER THIRTEEN

Access and Diversity

By Flora Mancuso Edwards

T HE COMMUNITY COLLEGE movement is the unique embodiment of one of the fundamental principles of American democracy. It's what makes us different from the rest of the world. It's that special principle that affirms that access to higher education is a fundamental right to be accorded to all, not a privilege to be bestowed only on those who have success guaranteed as a birthright. And that makes us very unusual.

Community colleges are the children of the post-industrial era. If we have a tradition, it's flexibility. We're the quick-change artists of higher education. We evolve and we change our missions; we keep responding to the different needs of our economic and demographic faces. There are probably not two or three of us that are really alike, because we belong to our localities. Our character is almost completely forged by the needs of the people and the communities we serve.

That's wonderful. It's noble. And it's certainly socially useful. But it's also out of sync with the rest of the higher education community.

Higher education has always used the commonality rather than the diversity of interests to maintain the sanctity of the ivory tower. Historically, the height of the tower and the density of the ivy were usually sufficient to ensure the homogeneity and the safety of the academic community.

Then something happened. The combined forces of demography, technology, and economics did what our commitment to social justice was unable to do. It shook us out of our complacency, and it demanded that we all look at our students in a brand new light. The face of America is changing, and we need to change with it.

Bud Hodgkinson tells us that "by around the year 2000, America will be a nation in which one of every three of us will be non-White. Minorities will cover a broader socioeconomic range than ever before, making simplistic treatment of their needs even less useful. By 1992, half of our college-age students will be over twenty-five, and 20 percent will be over thirty-five." Whether that new population is distinguished by age, ethnicity, sex, or ability, we must respond or fail. And for us in the community college, what we do from here on in is going to be very, very important.

We do not have the luxury of opting not to respond to changing demographics. These are our students. Our only claim to credibility is the quality of our output, because we don't screen the quality of our input. As open-access institutions, we can't hide behind SAT scores, prohibitive tuition rates, or admission committees. These new, diverse populations are here. They have to succeed, or we will fail as institutions.

Our success or failure is going to determine the shape of American society for years to come. This is the challenge of the decade, because unless we're ready to speak about a genuine institutional response to our new students—our minority students—the fabric of American higher education will never be made whole. A campus climate that can break down the barriers of color and caste has dealt with the greatest challenge facing American society. The rest is going to be easy by comparison.

Let's take a look at our campuses through the eyes of our minority students. I'm not too concerned about recruiting minority students; we have minority students. I'm concerned about what we do with them once we get them.

What do our minority students find as they pass through our campus gates? My fear is that on all too many of our campuses, no matter how few or numerous they are, minority students find themselves unnoticed and invisible in the classroom, in the curriculum, and in the extracurricular life of the college. Sometimes they pass like shadows in the night, dwindling in number, lost in a complacent world that never even saw them go. We can blame all kinds of external factors—financial aid policy, the economy, and other social inequities—but there is a lot that we can do right on campus to keep minority students from falling through the cracks.

The Four C's of Institutional Change

Consider the four C's of institutional change: commitment, community, curriculum, and the classroom.

Institutional commitment, or lack of it, is communicated in a hundred places in a thousand different ways. We see it in our cafeterias, in our lecture halls, in our residence halls, in faculty offices, in classrooms, in our board rooms. It's a question of institutional tone, and it sets the stage for all of our programmatic and curricular responses. It's not a policy statement; it's an expression of vision. If we find intolerance abhorrent, then we have to say so very loudly from the top, and we have to say so often.

If we profess that we're concerned about what we're teaching, then regardless of the subject matter, we need to teach respect. Stop using words like tolerance, because tolerance erodes very quickly as times get tough. We need to talk about diversity as a resource to be treasured, not as a problem to be dealt with. We also have to express our commitment through an institutional response that accommodates some of the economic and personal emergencies that many of our students face. We have to start rethinking our definitions of family, of resource, of responsibility.

We have to take the show on the road. We have to stop saying we can do it alone. Every student that we lose is a student lost to the economy, and there is an industry somewhere that will be hurt. We do not have to go to industry hat in hand; we have to go to industry with a prospectus, something their stockholders should be very interested in, because that's what's going to turn their wheels of progress now and in the future. If they're serious, they'll help us. They'll provide role models. They'll help us structure smooth college career transitions. They'll do all those things; they'll invest not just money, but also time and effort so that the light at the end of the tunnel for our students doesn't seem so far away.

Then we have to look at those students who aren't thinking about the light at the end of the tunnel—those students who are still looking for the tunnel. We need to examine our support services and reshape them as an integrated package, anticipating the needs of our students in an alien environment. We need to provide constructive intervention before it turns into crisis intervention, because crisis intervention rarely is timely enough to be useful. That's commitment.

Second, we also need to broaden our definition of community. We need to critically examine the academic community that we've created and ask ourselves if we're not telling our minority students that by virtue of their under-representation, and in some cases invisibility, certain fields of study are off-limits.

Students who see themselves reflected in no other place than the educational opportunity center draw some very sad conclusions about how realistic their own hopes and aspirations are. Just as important, faculty who regard a minority colleague as an anthropological oddity draw equally sad conclusions about the potential and the ability of their minority students. There's only so much we can accomplish by talking. At some point, we really have to start doing, and to do, we need some living examples.

As an academic community, we have to recognize that the whole really is more than the sum of its parts. Access is promoted or impeded by the gestalt that makes up the campus community. It's not one, two, or three things. Access is a program of co-curricular activities that broadens our cultural perspectives rather than reinforces comfortable models. Access is providing meaningful opportunities for students of all backgrounds to work together, to contribute to communities different from their own.

Finally, if we are going to commit ourselves academically to change, then we have to look at the whole package, and that includes the curriculum.

The curriculum is always the hardest nut to crack, and we're never quite sure how to do it. Usually, our curriculum is discipline-oriented; it's driven by an accepted body of literature; it doesn't have much room for more than passing acknowledgement of alternative values, alternative histories, and alternative cultures. The result is that the Afro-centric or the Hispanic perspective is ghettoized into departments that are appropriately labeled. That does two things: it isolates our minority students; and it robs majority students and faculty of a very important perspective in a world that is shrinking.

So if we're going to change it, we need to make a serious academic commitment to ask some questions about what we teach; about what common values are shared and reinforced across the curriculum; about what models of heroism we provide; about what room we have for diversity; and how we promote and recognize scholarship on emerging topics.

Of one thing I am certain: just as the impetus must begin at the top, the programmatic response has to begin in the classroom. Every semester, I teach. I have taught all my life, because it's one of the most sacred things that anyone can do. You can build a Taj Mahal, and if what's happening in the classroom isn't meaningful, all you have is a monument to mediocrity.

We don't need to throw out the traditional organization of the academy. It works as well as any other. What we need is to commit the time and resources to provide our faculties with structured opportunities to consider the non-Western world from the perspective of their own discipline. We need to make a commitment to cultural literacy that E.D. Hirsch never envisioned.

All of these are serious commitments. Each involves investment and risk. But if we in higher education like to think of ourselves as the architects of that next generation, then we'd better have a program that's characterized by something other than inertia.

This is a good time for us to remember that we who make up the educational enterprise are not charged with merely reflecting the world, but with improving it. Our success or failure in responding to our nation's minorities in many ways is going to be the measure of our worth.

Flora Mancuso Edwards is president of Middlesex County College in Edison, New Jersey.

CHAPTER FOURTEEN

Institutional Effectiveness

By Richard Alfred

EFFECTIVENESS IS A hot topic in community colleges. It is no longer news that our institutions are under pressure to demonstrate results; the questions are, What is effectiveness and how do you measure it? Does a unique model exist that distinguishes community colleges from other institutions? Are criteria such as degree completion, transfer rates, and enrollment growth useful and appropriate indicators of effectiveness? What are the implications of effectiveness criteria for governance, management, and leadership? These questions were initially posed by community college practitioners in the early 1970s, but answers were not forthcoming.

Unfortunately, effectiveness is an emotionally charged word in many community colleges. Repeated attacks by critics in recent years have left faculty and administrators with jaundiced views of the concept. The central issue raised by the critics is the performance of two-year institutions in advancing students to higher levels of education and occupational achievement, thereby reducing social class discrepancies.

This issue has been expressed in several forms, two of which have gained more than a fair share of attention: the questionable legitimacy of community colleges because of their emphasis on vocational training programs; and the social and economic disparities induced by community colleges through program offerings that encourage low transfer rates.

In response, community college practitioners argue that the critics do not know what they are talking about because they have no practical experience upon which to base judgments and they focus on only a small part of what community colleges do, thereby lessening the value of their contributions.

Is there a realistic and meaningful concept of effectiveness in community colleges? Research shows us that effectiveness is closely associated with conceptualizations of institutions. That is, distinctions between the types of students served, programs, and funding sources are an inherent part of any view of what the institution is. Variation in conceptualizations of colleges and universities, therefore, leads to variation in models for effectiveness.

Perspectives on Effectiveness

All theories of organizations rely on some conception of differences between high-performing (effective) and low-performing (ineffective) institutions.

Empirically, effectiveness is generally the ultimate dependent variable in research on community colleges.

Strategically, changes are occurring in the fabric of American social institutions that urge adaptability on the part of community colleges. Forces such as the decline of U.S. supremacy in world and domestic markets, economic uncertainty, structural change in the family, advancing technology, and changing public attitudes demand institutional responses. Community colleges failing to effectively address the relationship of institutional programs to changing societal forces will face performance criticism.

Pragmatically, students, parents, elected officials, business and industry officials, and other major stockholders in higher education are continually faced with making judgments about effectiveness. As they make choices concerning whether and where to attend college, how much money to allocate, what programs to develop, or which graduates to hire, they invariably inject information about effectiveness into the judgment equation. This information may be obtained through direct contact with the college or through conversations with friends, newspapers, or college publications. Whatever the method, the choices made by individuals are inherently tied to judgments of effectiveness.

Despite the centrality of effectiveness, confusion and ambiguity characterize efforts to manage and improve it. There are multiple perspectives.

For example, we can view effectiveness from an inside-out perspective in which institutional traditions and staff preferences determine how it is defined and measured. Some inside-out perspectives are:

• The extent to which the college achieves its stated mission and goals (mission and goal achievement)

• The absence of faults, problems, or other signs of weakness that make the institution ineffective (smooth functioning)

• The acquisition of human and financial resources that increase the size of the college and make it more visible (bigger is better)

• High satisfaction among faculty and staff with all constituencies at least minimally satisfied (staff satisfaction)

• The reputation of the college relative to other similar organizations (competitive advantage)

We can also view effectiveness from the vantage point of individuals and groups outside of the college. This is the outside-in perspective. Some examples are:

• Clarity in the stated mission and goals leading to public acceptance and support (mission clarity)

• Programs and services offered on a timely basis that satisfy important needs (constituency satisfaction)

• Educational outcomes that are valued by important constituencies, especially resource providers (student outcomes)

• Marketing strategies using student outcomes information that convey an image of success to specific audiences (effective communication)

In the 1990s, outside-in will become the dominant conception of effectiveness in community colleges. The comprehensive mission and vaguely expressed purposes of our colleges make it easy for external groups to equate personal preferences with effectiveness. Business and industry employers, elected officials, and other funders will receive greater attention as the need for operating resources grows. Hence, performance indicators such as the relationship of jobs to curriculum, job skills, and employer satisfaction will rise to the top in effectiveness evaluations.

Most institutions are not organized to evaluate and improve effectiveness using the outside-in approach. Community colleges have limited their examinations of effectiveness to simple accounts of mission and goal achievement, the pace of growth, and the use of services and facilities. These are inside-out indicators. They are not sufficient to evaluate performance at a time when the public is evaluating value received for the dollar. Community colleges need to take a fresh look at effectiveness, beginning with how it is defined, its dimensions, and criteria for measurement.

The Paradox of Effectiveness

An attribute of central importance to American higher education is its diversity. Differences exist among institutions. These differences lead to variation in the criteria for effectiveness. As client-centered institutions, community colleges employ a wide variety of programs and services in a compact region to meet the needs of diverse groups. Like other service organizations, they are effective when individuals and groups hold favorable perceptions of their performance in important activities or successful organizational transactions. Transactions differ, however, according to the needs of each group, and a successful transaction for one group may not be successful for another.

It is precisely this point that identifies some of the most important findings about community college effectiveness in research recently completed at the University of Michigan. These findings can be summarized as follows: Effectiveness in community colleges is determined by the presence of paradox.

Paradox exists when colleges employ simultaneously contradictory programs, practices, and delivery systems to respond to groups holding different expectations. To illustrate, faculty and students holding traditional academic values may view effectiveness as attainment of the associate degree or continuing study toward advanced degrees. For work-related groups such as business and industry employers, effectiveness may mean students enroll in one or more courses to update job skills. For policy makers concerned about cost-benefits, effectiveness may mean documented outcomes achieved at the lowest possible cost. Finally, policy-making groups such as executive administrators and trustees may view effectiveness in terms of management practices that facilitate growth, bring the institution into closer contact with the community, and/or maximize efficiency in the use of resources.

This tells us that effectiveness is in the eye of the beholder. It is a product of two P's: performance and perception. Community colleges are effective when important groups hold favorable perceptions of their performance. To become effective, they must employ a variety of programs, practices, and delivery systems to meet important needs. To improve effectiveness, they must systematically inform themselves about constituency perceptions and apply this information to performance.

Three questions command our attention: What are the attributes of paradox in community colleges? How do they contribute to effectiveness? What are the implications of paradox for important activities such as governance, teaching and learning, and leadership?

Research carried out at the University of Michigan in 1989 involving 2,410 faculty, trustees, and administrators from community colleges throughout the nation led to the identification of eight attributes of paradox. These are:

1. Mission comprehensiveness—which permits the simultaneous pursuit of contradictory goals—along with mission specificity—which permits concentration on selected goals undertaken with specific groups. More than one-half (55 percent) of the faculty, administrators, and trustees viewed the institutional mission as comprehensive, involving the simultaneous pursuit of contradictory, equally important goals such as access, public service, excellence, and human resource development. Conversely, a significant number viewed a specific goal as more important than the rest. Effective community colleges are simultaneously oriented toward a comprehensive mission that permits wide latitude in adapting to the environment and also toward a specific mission that allows them to focus on the special needs of particular groups.

2. Open-door admissions—which promote access and opportunity—and selective admissions—which promote excellence and program quality. A majority (82 percent) of faculty and administrators described admissions policies as simultaneously oriented toward opening the door to diverse learners and limiting access by establishing entrance standards for specific programs. Effective community colleges emphasize quality in programs, but at the same time they are market-sensitive and reactive to the needs of diverse students. Less effective institutions have staff that lose sight of the need to establish and maintain quality in programs. On the other hand, emphasizing quality at the expense of adapting to student needs and market conditions inhibits effectiveness.

3. Emphasis on technical education—which promotes links between education and work, skill training, and currency—as well as emphasis on liberal arts education—which promotes flexibility, critical thinking, and historical perspective. The vast majority (96 percent) of the respondents in the study described the primary curriculum objective for the general student population as a combination of technical, liberal arts, and life skills education. Effective

community colleges emphasize and reinforce the value of the liberal arts, while at the same time emphasizing linkages between education and work through technical training. The necessity for marketable skills and state-of-the-art training exists simultaneously with the requirement for critical thinking and transferrable skills needed to adapt to change.

4. Nontraditional delivery systems—which foster new perspectives and innovation in the delivery of services and facilitate developing outreach programs—as well as traditional delivery systems—which foster commitment to past strategies involving traditional definitions of the semester and credit hour. Overwhelmingly, the major delivery system involves a combination of traditional and nontraditional strategies. Over one-half (58 percent) of the faculty, administrators, and trustees indicated that a combination of campus- and community-based strategies were used to deliver services. Rapidly changing conditions act as stimuli for the development of nontraditional community-based delivery systems, while static conditions support the need for traditional campus-based delivery systems.

5. Planned change—which encourages wide search, careful consideration of innovations, and adherence to a plan in developing new programs—as well as spontaneous change—which encourages quick execution and flexibility in developing programs. Over one-third (36 percent) of the faculty, administrators, and trustees believed that their institutions were simultaneously liberal and conservative in pursuing innovations to adapt to changing needs and conditions. Effective community colleges engage in proactive, entrepreneurial, and innovative activities that contribute to short-term success in meeting market needs. Simultaneously, they enact conservative planning and budgeting mechanisms (efficiency measures) oriented toward long-term survival.

6. Breadth and variety in the definition of student success—which reinforces the comprehensive mission—as well as specificity in the interpretation of student success to different groups and organizations—which reinforces the capacity of community colleges to meet the needs of specific markets. Beyond any doubt, community colleges emphasize the comprehensive nature of student outcomes. More than three-quarters (82 percent) of the faculty, administrators, and trustees indicated that a combination of different outcomes such as enrollment without plans for a degree, associate degree completion, transfer, baccalaureate degree completion, job entry, etc., were not sufficient, in and of themselves, to describe success. Community colleges broadly define student outcomes in order to reinforce their comprehensive mission, while at the same time pointing to specific outcomes as evidence of their ability to meet special needs.

7. Quantitative conceptions of academic quality—which foster assessment of performance using obtrusive measures—as well as qualitative conceptions—which foster discreet approaches to performance assessment. In the University of Michigan study, more than three-quarters (80 percent) of the respondents said that their institution uses both quantitative and qualitative factors to define quality. Faculty, administrators, and trustees pay a great deal of attention to

symbols as well as substance. On the one hand, discrete indicators such as student learning outcomes, public opinion, and teaching ability of faculty are instituted so that assessment can be made of the extent to which the basic mission is achieved. On the other hand, substance is ignored in favor of image. A great deal of attention is paid to indicators of institutional size (enrollment, budget, facilities, etc.) to help constituencies interpret institutional performance favorably. The capacity of faculty and administrators to manage symbols and interpretations effectively is a critical difference between effective institutions and those that are not effective.

8. Externally initiated linkages with community organizations—which reinforce dependence, immediacy, and service of needs—as well as internally initiated linkages with community organizations—which reinforce autonomy, planning, and mission integrity. More than eight out of ten respondents (82 percent) indicated that varied strategies were used for initiating partnerships with community organizations depending on the situation and conditions inside and outside of the institution. Administrators simultaneously respond to external needs and safeguard institutional autonomy by concentrating on campus governance and strategic planning. In this way community colleges insulate the institution against the encroachment of external groups and organizations, and at the same time initiate aggressive strategies to influence the external environment and important publics.

Without the tension that exists between simultaneous opposites—what we have called paradox—unproductive narrowing would occur. Narrowing is a process in which one activity in a community college is perpetrated in extreme, thereby reducing the emphasis on other activities. For example, if interest in transfer and baccalaureate degree completion as the measure of student success is allowed to dominate a college's attention, there will be diminished interest in other forms of success (e.g., job attainment, personal satisfaction, job upgrading). This, in turn, reinforces even more interest in transfer and baccalaureate degree completion and less interest in other forms of success.

Accordingly, narrowing the criteria for measuring student success to transfer and baccalaureate degree completion undermines the comprehensive mission of community colleges. Unless a paradoxical condition exists in which simultaneously contradictory, equally compelling interpretations of student success are accepted and used, dysfunctional cycles emerge that could lead to ineffectiveness. One interpretation of success would overshadow others until the institution becomes so out of balance that its mission must be altered or refocused to improve effectiveness.

Looking to the Future

Although community colleges, as flexible, multipurpose institutions, are seemingly well-equipped to meet the needs of different constituencies, a fundamental question remains. Are we organized to improve effectiveness? Through the way we plan, make decisions, and allocate resources, will we adapt to change in the future as well as we have in the past? Are we using human resources to contribute to effectiveness?

Information collected in the University of Michigan study revealed potential disparities between the comprehensive, multipurpose nature of community colleges and their internal organization. Community colleges appear to operate as closed systems not fully in touch with their environment. Planning is conducted in a vacuum, decisions are made by a few at the top, and assessment is limited to occasional studies of student outcomes based on institutional convenience.

Organizational theory informs us that in periods of turbulence, adaptive institutions are organized as open systems. As open systems, community colleges encourage faculty and staff to interpret the environment and to participate in decisions, thereby leading them to contribute more energy to the institution. In a closed system, community colleges focus more carefully on the pursuit of internally defined goals, with faculty and staff acting in accordance with organizational desires advanced by leaders. Motivation suffers when participation in decision making is constrained. As motivation declines, the staff withdraws its support from the institution and diminishes the college's ability to adapt.

One can argue, then, that staff involvement in planning and decision making is an important ingredient in community college effectiveness. This ingredient is present in a college whose staff work together to map the future through planning. That is, at different levels in the organization, faculty and administrators come together to scan the environment, assess institutional performance, and identify priorities.

Overemphasis on control by a few at the top of an organization can produce stagnation, frustration, and loss of morale. This situation can be observed routinely in community colleges where administrators make top-down decisions and seek input from a few specific staff members. On the other hand, random participation of faculty and staff in planning and decision making can create confusion, wasted effort, and a loss of direction. It is balance between participation and control in a carefully considered administrative structure that empowers community colleges to adapt to the environment.

This balance is not in place in many community colleges. Too many have administrators who are interested in building linkages with community organizations but who have lost sight of the need to more fully use the college's own human resources. Community colleges desiring to become more effective must find ways to accentuate paradox using the full resources available to the institution. This can be accomplished through fundamental changes in management and governance.

Management and Governance. Having been propelled for nearly three decades by growth, our colleges have taken on the image of high-achieving service institutions. This image has both pluses and minuses. On the plus side, growth as a measure of success is easy to document and communicate to external groups. On the minus side, continuous emphasis on growth constrains the need for planning. Lacking data about trends in the environment and college performance, leaders choose to maintain breadth in the college's programs and services as insurance against the potential effects of change. This is expensive in terms of dollars and human resources. It means more programs, more services, more staff, and a higher fixed-cost commitment.

Community colleges seriously interested in improving effectiveness engage in planning. Planning worthy of the name empowers faculty and administrators to identify forces and trends in the environment that require change in order for their institution to adapt. Adding new programs and services, retooling and deleting old ones, changing program priorities—these are the changes that bring our colleges into line with their environments. They reinforce paradox by freeing up resources or adding new resources that enable programs to turn on a dime as market conditions dictate.

To be worthwhile, planning must be done at all organizational levels and must involve those who will implement policies, develop programs, and teach classes. Effective colleges will implement systems for continuous environmental scanning, performance assessment, and planning at all levels. In the process, faculty roles and workloads will change. Tomorrow's faculty members will do more than teach. They will forecast market conditions, plan and evaluate curricula, conduct research on student outcomes, build marketing and recruitment plans, lobby private-sector markets for resources, and perform other management functions as necessary to improve program performance. Collective bargaining contracts will be rewritten to simultaneously change the nature of faculty workload and maintain continuity in faculty and administrator roles.

Assessment. While the Michigan study revealed general agreement concerning the need for more entry and exit assessment of students, there are some who view assessment as costly. Simply put, they feel that the time, dollars, and expertise required may exceed the benefits. Such a one-dimensional view reflects little recognition or understanding of the importance of information about student aptitudes, performance, and outcomes in planning and decision making. This assumption needs to be challenged directly in our colleges.

Colleges that define effectiveness in terms of the presence of paradox are complex in purpose and performance. To build understanding and support among constituencies, they need to be cognizant of student outcomes, the relationship of these outcomes to aptitudes at entry, and the overall benefits of college attendance. Not only must our colleges be aware of their effects on students, but they must also be able to view these effects from the perspective of different groups.

To improve effectiveness, we need to build assessment programs that ask and answer important questions. Some of these questions are:

- What is the societal context for student outcomes?
    —How many and what types of jobs will require a certificate, an associate degree, a baccalaureate degree?
    —For which students are academic degrees necessary and appropriate?
    —How do trends in technology, the economy, and the work force affect student educational and career goals?
- What are the educational and career goals of entering students?
    —How many students plan to obtain a certificate or associate degree?
    —How many students plan to transfer, to complete a baccalaureate degree or advanced degree?
- How many and what types of students transfer or graduate with a certificate or an associate degree?
- What near-term outcomes (one to three years) and long-term outcomes (more than three years) do community colleges produce with students interested in work and those desiring to further their education?
- What is the level of satisfaction among different groups (alumni, business and industry, four-year college faculty and administrators, elected officials, etc.) with the outcomes of community college education?

These are the types of questions that our colleges must address in the coming years. Many institutions have begun to think ahead in anticipating calls for information about student success. But assessment programs have yet to be developed that will consistently yield information precisely and comprehensively enough to satisfy important audiences.

Leadership. The next generation of community college leaders will have toiled in specialized roles beneath the president over a period of years before assuming the CEO role. For this reason, their understanding of organizational dynamics may be fragmented. They may have a greater tendency to see the college as a collection of pieces, and they may lack a global understanding of the community college as a social institution.

The impact of specialization will be felt throughout our colleges. It will affect curriculum, enrollment, and public affairs policies as well as financial management. Leaders lacking a conceptual understanding will experience difficulty in positioning institutions for maximum gain with constituencies. They will also be vulnerable to critics who use personalized conceptions of the community college as a platform from which to evaluate effectiveness.

What can our colleges do to neutralize the negative effects of specialization and the prospect that the next generation of leaders may not be able to perform to an expected level? There are strategies for leader preparation that make a difference. Indeed, strategic thinking applied to the development of leaders has never been more important than at present because all institutions are vulnerable. A college at which effectiveness is dependent on paradox must have leaders who can communicate in language easily understood by the public.

While a supply of leaders with conceptual and communication skills will exist in the future, it will be a small supply.

There are many strategies that can be used to develop leaders with these skills:

• Introduce future leaders to concepts of organizational behavior, dynamics, and culture at an early stage in their careers. Community colleges are unique in mission, service region, and institutional/environmental linkages. They need to be understood as such by those in leadership positions. Expecting leaders to understand this uniqueness by virtue of experience without exposure to important general theories in the social sciences may be unrealistic. There is a role for graduate education in the preparation of community college leaders.

• Emphasize to leaders the importance of institutional culture and historical antecedents of culture. There has been much criticism about leaders who make changes without understanding the culture of the institution and how it evolved over time. Leaders who understand how effectiveness works and who have the capacity to improve effectiveness will be firmly grounded in the culture of the institution.

• Avoid the harmful effects of specialization by exposing leaders to the broad scale of community college operations at an early point in their careers. This can be accomplished through staff development, mentoring, job rotation, etc. The important thing is that it is done.

• Increase awareness of the implications (for effectiveness) of a comprehensive mission by providing opportunities for leaders to interact with important publics at an early stage in their development. Close contact with groups holding different values and expectations for community college education will undoubtedly sensitize them to the different ways that effectiveness can be interpreted. It will also guide them in efforts to manage and improve effectiveness through understanding paradox.

None of these recommendations calls for drastic changes in current methods and strategies for leader development; rather they are aimed at the more systematic exposure of leaders to the factors that determine institutional effectiveness. They take into account the unique context for community college education and the role of leaders in interpreting the institution to important publics.

Words such as change and turbulence describe the environment for the coming decade. This is a time for community colleges to build and operate meaningful interpretations of effectiveness and to communicate them to the public.

It is certainly not a time to accede to narrow interpretations of performance that misrepresent the comprehensive mission, however strong the critics' claims. Nor is it a time for conducting haphazard assessment of institutional performance that does not take into account fundamental principles upon which our colleges are organized. This is a watershed time when the future of many a community college could be profoundly affected both by conditions in the environment and the way in which the public interprets them.

Colleges can take steps to improve effectiveness. Viewing effective performance as linked to the presence of paradox, we can organize our colleges to manage through improved systems of management, governance, and assessment. We can also do a better job of preparing leaders. Moving performance assessment as far down in the organization as possible may well be the most important challenge for improving effectiveness. We must constantly pose the question—What constitutes effective performance?—and then put into place programs, services, and delivery systems that will help answer it. This is an ongoing process, one that requires a meaningful conception of effectiveness. The work has just begun.

Richard Alfred is an associate professor at the University of Michigan in Ann Arbor, Michigan, and co-director of the Community College Consortium.

CHAPTER FIFTEEN

Faculty and Administrative Renewal

By George B. Vaughan

A S THE NATION prepares for the twenty-first century, one major policy question facing America's community colleges is how to identify, develop, and maintain faculty members and administrators who are intellectually vibrant and who understand and are committed to the mission of the public community college. These administrators and faculty should be—must be—leaders with the vision to shape the mission in a way that allows the community college to respond to current societal needs and to anticipate what these needs may be in the future.

Those currently in leadership positions must view their roles from a different perspective, a perspective that considers professional renewal to be not only a right, but also an obligation of every faculty member and administrator.

Why is faculty and administrative vitality so important at this time, and why am I suggesting that long-range planning include ways of maintaining and enhancing faculty and administrative leadership?

I suggest that new and vigorous leadership is required at this particular point in time for the following reasons: (1) aging faculty and administrators, many of whom played key roles in founding community colleges and who have continued to provide that "spark of mission" for younger community college professionals, are retiring; (2) faculty members and administrators new to the community college often lack the devotion to a "sense of mission" that characterized the founding groups; (3) new faculty and administrative positions are currently difficult to obtain, thus closing the door to renewal provided in the past by moving from one campus to another; (4) the large number of part-time faculty employed at most colleges makes it difficult to develop a sense of mission and a sense of community on many campuses; (5) unions, while increasing benefits on some campuses, have failed to help create the collegiality that is needed to keep professionals intellectually stimulated; (6) in many cases, community college presidents have failed to provide the intellectual leadership that must be present if members of the college community are to achieve their potential; (7) while community college enrollments are uncertain for the future, we know that the number of traditional college-age students will begin to increase in the mid-1990s; and (8) it is projected that there will be a dearth of faculty members at all levels of higher education by the end of the century, resulting in competition among higher education institutions for faculty in all disciplines.

New positions will not necessarily take us back to the days of musical chairs when moving was a major avenue for renewal. When faculty vacancies again occur, many of the colleges will seek younger, less expensive faculty to fill them; moreover, existing faculty and administrators with families, low interest rate mortgages, children in high school, investments in a retirement system, and birthday number 50 staring them in the eyes are unready or unwilling to move. All of the above reasons cry out for professional renewal, a top priority for community colleges now and in the future.

I offer three suggestions for dealing with the always complex and often emotional issue of faculty and administrative vibrancy: teaching faculty members must occupy a more prominent role in providing collegewide leadership; community college professionals, including teaching faculty, student services professionals, learning resource professionals, and administrators—specifically deans and presidents—must rededicate or, in many cases, dedicate themselves to the pursuit of scholarship; and part-time faculty must be used more effectively and more professionally.

Faculty as Leaders

Teaching faculty members must occupy a more prominent role in providing collegewide leadership. In the past we have relied almost totally on administrative leadership in planning the direction of our colleges and have not made faculty members full partners in the enterprise. To rely almost totally on administrators to lead the community college into the next century is to view the issues too narrowly and to define leadership too traditionally and too exclusively.

If faculty members are to move into the mainstream of college leadership, they cannot remain indifferent to the larger aims of education. To lead, faculty must be informed; to be informed requires broad reading not only in the disciplines, but also in the field of higher education. On the other hand, deans and presidents must not only invite teaching faculty members to sit at the table once the meal is ready to be consumed, but also involve faculty in helping to decide what meal is to be prepared, when, by whom, and in what form. Teaching faculty must be involved as our colleges grapple with such issues as the role of the community college in international education, in adult literacy, in defining and enhancing technological literacy, in working with an aging population, in promoting the humanities, and in dealing with any number of issues you care to list.

Why must teaching faculty members play key leadership roles? They can bring experience, knowledge, and compassion to the leadership of the college that will be missing if they are excluded. For example, how many colleges have ever involved language and economics teachers in the debate on the role of the community college in international education? Philosophy and sociology teachers as well as teachers in engineering technology must discuss the role of the community college in promoting "technological literacy." Nursing

108

faculty and counselors should be intimately involved in planning educational programs for an aging population, including programs devoted to physical and mental health. As drugs and alcohol continue to devour our young and not-so-young, college counselors must understand that these problems are societal problems and that the individual student is a victim, not necessarily a cause of this plague. Librarians and other members of learning resource divisions can be indispensable to a college grappling with how to process and communicate information.

A word of caution is in order: Faculty involvement in helping to lead the college is one side of a two-sided coin, with administrators on the other side, a situation that has some potential problems as well as solutions. Administrators must be willing to involve faculty in ways that go beyond the illusion of faculty leadership that currently exists on too many campuses. On the other hand, faculty must view the issues facing community colleges as extending beyond higher salaries and lower teaching loads, for professionals do not live by bread or release time alone. Teaching faculty must view their role and the role of their teaching field as encompassing more than imparting knowledge in the classroom. Faculty members must cross the boundaries that separate their discipline and their role as classroom teachers from the larger issues facing higher education and in turn see education and themselves as being a part of a picture much larger than themselves. Indeed, in the future our vision must encompass the world as we attempt to understand different people and different problems.

Scholarship and the Community College Professional

In contemplating the future, a second consideration must be the role of scholarship in the revitalization of community college professionals. It is gratifying to see that the report of the AACJC Commission on the Future of Community Colleges spoke to the need for community college professionals to be scholars. The report reminds us that each community college professional needs to be a dedicated scholar. For this to become a reality, the meaning of scholarship must be broadened.

As we continue to evaluate and define the role our colleges are to play in our own professional lives and in the lives of our community, we must realize that the failure to include scholarship as an important element in the community college philosophy—in our long-range plans—is a flaw that erodes the vitality and effectiveness of the community college professional. I agree with the commission's report that all community college professionals should be scholars, for it is through scholarship that a disciplined love for learning manifests itself. Scholarship is the avenue through which we stay in touch with the academic enterprise; it constantly pulls us back to learning, back to the college's mission, back to the core of the enterprise.

Scholarship gives us legitimacy in the world of higher education. Scholarship is truly the coin of the realm in our profession, for without it we might as well be working at the local bank or department store. However, we must engage in scholarship in a way that is relevant to the community college. Taking the commission's advice, an important step in the right direction is defining what we mean by scholarship.

I offer this definition for your consideration:

Scholarship is the systematic pursuit of a topic, an objective, rational inquiry that involves critical analysis. It requires the precise observing, organizing, and recording of information in the search for truth and order. Scholarship is the umbrella under which research falls, for research is but one form of scholarship. Scholarship results in a product that is shared with others and that is subject to the criticism of individuals qualified to judge the product. This product may take the form of a book review, an annotated bibliography, a lecture, a review of existing research on a topic, a speech that is a synthesis of the thinking on a topic. Scholarship requires that one have a solid foundation in one's professional field and that one keep up with the developments in that field.

The Use of Part-Time Faculty

The third suggestion I offer for maintaining intellectually vibrant faculty and administrators is the effective recruitment, use, and professionalization of part-time faculty. I realize that this may well be the most difficult task among the three. Nevertheless, the use of part-time faculty is an issue that must be included in your long-range plan if you are to develop and maintain a truly vibrant faculty and administration.

We should cease using the term "part-time faculty" generically. Rather, we need to view part-time faculty in terms of their goals, in conjunction with the goals of the institution. Realizing that describing part-time faculty is more difficult than placing them in categories, we should think of part-time faculty as members of one of two categories.

Category one part-time faculty members are not interested in full-time teaching as a career, unless they are already teaching in high school or a similar institution. I refer to them as independents because their income and therefore their livelihoods are independent of the income they receive as part-time teachers at the community college. Neither their professional nor social lives are tied closely to the college.

They teach because they enjoy performing; they teach because it satisfies the ego; they teach as a way of fulfilling their civic duty; and they teach because they believe in the community college mission. Falling into this group are lawyers, bankers, dentists and doctors, business executives, master crafts-men and technicians, politicians, actors, writers, and high school teachers, al-though unfortunately the latter group may do it for the money or as a means of getting their foot into the community college's door rather than for more altruistic reasons. Members of this group are not going to commit a great deal of time to attending faculty meetings, serving on committees, or doing any of the other things that are expected of full-time faculty members. Members of this group are unlikely to protest decisions by the administration or the low pay they receive for their services.

The more interesting group to deal with, and those who I believe should receive serious consideration in your long-range plan (because they have the potential to bring the most to the college community), I refer to as the de-pendents. Members of this group are committed to teaching as a career and wish to pursue it full-time. They depend upon the income they receive from teaching part-time. While they are rarely accepted as full members of the col-lege community, they nevertheless fulfill many of their professional and social needs through their affiliation with the college. They find lingering on the periphery of the academic mainstream frustrating. Their career goal is often to join the community college faculty as a full-time member.

The dependents are often individuals who are working on or have a Ph.D. in low-demand disciplines such as the humanities and social sciences. This group makes up the itinerants of higher education, moving in and out of colleges as the opportunity presents itself. They have flexible schedules and are willing to teach anytime, anywhere, if it will advance them toward their goal of ob-taining a full-time teaching position. Members of this group are likely to show up at faculty meetings and are likely to protest the low salaries and working conditions of part-time faculty.

It is a mistake to view part-time faculty as a homogeneous group. While they have some things in common—they all want a desk, office space, recog-nition, and other amenities normally associated with teaching—the dependents make up the group that should be considered most carefully in long-range planning.

The dependents are potential academic revolutionaries. And why not? They are highly intelligent individuals, often possessing advanced degrees to which they have devoted three, four, or five years of their lives. They feel used by the system.

How can community colleges better serve part-time faculty and in turn better serve themselves?

• First and foremost, the two categories should be recognized and dealt with in different ways.

• Both groups should be provided with the basics such as office space. These basics are especially important to the dependents, who may well spend much of their day at the college.

- More effort should be made to bring the dependents into the mainstream of college activities. For example, most members of this group would welcome the opportunity to serve on college committees such as the curriculum committee. (In contrast, independents such as the bank executive would balk at such a suggestion.)
- You should recognize that by involving the dependents more in college activities, the line between part-time and full-time faculty will become blurred.
- You should be sensitive to how important financial rewards are to the dependents, and much more so than to the independents. Some means of rewarding the dependents must be devised. It may be necessary and desirable to define a faculty member's workload in terms of something other than teaching, thereby creating a rational way of paying dependent part-time faculty for work on college committees, for advising students, and for other activities that go beyond the classroom but are clearly activities that should be performed by professionals.
- We must all recognize that the community college of the future will likely continue to depend upon part-time faculty. These faculty members have, for the most part, been a good professional and financial investment in the past; therefore, it follows that their value to the college could be increased by additional duties and additional financial rewards.
- Finally, administrators and full-time faculty should exert a special effort to make the dependents feel that they are important colleagues who are just biding their time until they become full participants in the academic enterprise.

George B. Vaughan is the director of the Center for Community College Education at George Mason University in Fairfax, Virginia.

CHAPTER SIXTEEN

Assessment and Success

By James L. Wattenbarger

IF I WOULD make a little rhyme, it would be that "The research that is needed should be heeded." We've talked a great deal about the road to quality, and some who were around before 1945 will remember those days before television, before penicillin, before polio shots, before frozen food. There were no photocopies, there was no plastic. We didn't have contact lenses. Nobody knew what a Frisbee was, and we hadn't even heard of the Pill—although we sometimes wished for it. We grew up before radar, before credit cards. There weren't split atoms, laser beams, or ballpoint pens. We didn't have pantyhose, dishwashers, clothes dryers, electric blankets, and air conditioners. Drip-dry clothes were not thought of, and man never had walked on the moon.

All these devices came from research, and you can see how your life has changed. What would life be without ballpoint pens and pantyhose—or even dishwashers? In the field of education, however, we conduct research and then we often ignore it completely. We make decisions based solely on conventional wisdom. The people who make these decisions are intervening legislators and intervening governors, but sometimes even our college presidents and faculties do the same thing. If you've ever been to a faculty meeting and listened to the arguments, you may hear people make the most outlandish statements that they can't possibly prove—it's purely conventional wisdom, and it has nothing to do with good research.

About ten years ago, the Southern Regional Education Board (SREB) adopted a Report Card on the road to quality. It had a great deal of effect on the legislatures of many Southern states. According to the SREB report, in order to have quality in education, we needed to raise high school academic standards and graduation requirements.

Florida passed a law, the RAISE Bill, which was designed to increase the requirements for graduation from high school. The Inter-Institutional Research Council, a part of the Institute of Higher Education at the University of Florida, is currently conducting a study to see what effect RAISE has had on students who have followed the required program. For the past seven years, those graduates have entered the community colleges and the universities. Keep in mind, however, RAISE was based on conventional wisdom—not on any real research.

Secondly, the SREB said we needed to raise college admissions standards. The theory for this recommendation is that the higher you place the bar on the high jump, the higher people will be able to jump. That works very well for track and field events in encouraging people to jump just a little bit higher, but there may be a limit somewhere along the line where people can't jump any higher.

The third item on the SREB list was the need to tighten teacher selection standards. Some states have tried to set up ways of developing better teachers. It hasn't occurred in many states, but one of the ways to develop teachers is to professionalize the profession by increasing salaries. However, this has not been proved by research either.

Fourth, SREB said that cooperation toward achieving the mutual objectives of higher education and the elementary and secondary programs should occur. This involves paying attention to the relationships between high schools and colleges.

About this same time, the Southern Association of Colleges and Schools re-examined the qualifications for membership and requirements for accreditation. The association gave a great deal of attention to the issue of achieving quality in higher education. The concern for maintaining and improving quality while preserving access and diversity is a concern that should be shared by all of our policy makers.

Some have talked about how we have cut back access, and I'm talking about how we have cut it back even further—perhaps unintentionally—in an attempt to raise quality. The goals that we have adopted in American higher education have been to promote educational equity, the diversity of students and staff, and excellence in teaching and learning. These three goals are worthy goals and ones to which the community colleges have given particular attention.

Community colleges have achieved a reputation for providing equity because they have made it possible to remove some of the barriers. We've also given attention in community colleges to excellence in teaching and learning. But we have not given much attention to providing as good a research base for these activities as we need to in order to make good decisions. Research is still weak in regard to learning how young people make decisions about their education, particularly those who are not enrolling in colleges and universities. Information about how they make these decisions is critical in developing programs and strategies to influence these decisions.

The most acceptable use of assessment in the current "press-to-test" rush should be improving the teaching-learning process—especially under the conditions of increased diversity of both students and faculty. The diversity we want should include diversity of learning style as well as diversity of other student characteristics.

However, we still need a useful topology of assessment uses and practices. We still lack research on the effects of various kinds of assessments on diverse students and faculty. We know that some people test well and other people do not. And yet, we really haven't discovered why it is true or how to do something about it. We need to know more about test bias and discrimination.

And we need to know more about student motivation when test results are not used for or against them in regard to their progress. The good and bad effects of assessment in access and diversity should be used to improve our practices and strategies.

The first step in giving attention to access is that colleges and universities should no longer be judged on the basis of the freshmen they enroll. We have some standards for quality in our state that are imposed by the state board of education. Would you believe that one of the standards for judging an institution's quality is the number of Merit Scholars it enrolls as freshmen? The community colleges are not particularly designed to enroll Merit Scholars as freshmen, and the University of Florida spends a great deal of its energies beating the bushes for them. And the University gets a good many of them; about 70 percent of the Merit Scholars in our state attend the University of Florida. But would you want to compare the University of Florida to Santa Fe Community College, for example, based on which one has the highest percentage of Merit Scholars? It sounds ridiculous, yet it is one of the indicators that is used.

The state of Florida even uses the average SAT scores as a measure of an institution's quality. So what? That really has nothing to do with the quality of the institution, when you get down to it.

In the history of community colleges, our commitment to articulation has been strong, particularly with the four-year institutions to which students transfer to complete their baccalaureate degrees. And we've had many studies focused on finding out how well students do when they finish community colleges. A number of studies at the Institute of Higher Education indicate that Florida community college students who transfer do an excellent job at the universities. If the university professors don't want to believe that in their conventional wisdom, there is very little we can do about changing closed minds.

One thing we have done at the University of Florida, however, is to point out at graduation ceremonies the awards made for scholarship. In the twenty-odd years I've been to graduation at our university, there has not been one where there wasn't at least one community college transfer student who was awarded a scholarship with a 4.0 average. So there's no question that the community college transfers have kept up with the university students at least in that area.

The related goal of educational equity is also something we need to be concerned about in the push for access. We should be particularly concerned about minority groups who are not attending college in the numbers they should.

Our average freshman at the University of Florida comes from a White household with an annual income of over $55,000, and comes from a family that has had a tradition of college graduation.

The first-generation college student does not come to the university except in very rare instances. These are the people who are underrepresented and those about whom we need to be concerned. They are also the ones we need to encourage in the community college. We must continue to make sure that there is access, equity, and excellence for all groups and not just for a certain part of our society.

In 1960 we believed that equity entailed little more than access, and that was achieved when entering freshmen displayed ethnic and other diversities. In the following years, we have begun to acknowledge that access is a hollow promise if students are unable to transfer to the university.

We've even conducted several national studies to determine what's happening to transfer students. We need research that will help us remove or reduce the barriers to college attendance. We need research that will help us describe the conditions for which we can compensate—such as the cultural factors, including language (particularly among our Hispanic populations), home and family conditions, and readiness to undertake college-level work, as well as the intervention strategies that we need in order to impact targeted enrollments.

The current term that community colleges are using to illustrate their concern for bringing in a lot of students who have not been touched before is "enrollment management." One of the ways in which enrollment management differs from pure marketing is that it recognizes target groups and certain strategies. If we can develop the strategies and the ways of approaching targeted individuals, then we can improve the whole process of enrollment management.

In 1983 one of my doctoral students examined Florida legislation that was passed between 1957 and 1981. Forty-one statutes pertained to five aspects of the open-door philosophy. And in most instances, the open-door philosophy deteriorated.

Henderson's findings in Florida noted that forty-eight laws relating to community colleges were passed during this twenty-five-year period, with most of the emphasis upon geographical and financial accessibility. The findings also noted that over 70 percent of the laws were concerned with these two aspects and that the least attention on the part of the legislature was placed on counseling services. Overall, the emphasis of these laws was upon actions affecting the provision of financial accessibility, the provision of geographic accessibility, and diversity of programs; little attention was paid to the commitment to serve all people beyond the basic legal commitments outlined in the original law.

One of the members of the House of Representatives in Florida has said that we've achieved access and now we need to be worried about quality, since access is no longer a problem. He hadn't looked at the statistics, but that's what he said. Hyde's report in 1982 on access doesn't support the assertion that access had been achieved. By defining access as a concept, Hyde pointed out that it should include removal of unequal barriers to attendance, whether geographical, financial, or informational.

A second barrier is found in a report on institutional climate. Many students say, "I just didn't feel welcome," or "I didn't feel I could study in this climate." It happens far too often, but colleges are not as much concerned about that as they should be.

A third barrier is the recognition that institutional sectors operate and are financially supported differently, that sometimes our liberal arts programs are financed on one basis, our vocational programs on another, and our continuing education on yet another. In fact, I've been working with colleges in Massachusetts where state funds are not provided to support anyone who attends after four o'clock in the afternoon. Now, I don't know what four o'clock has to do with it, but after that time of day, they get no money from the state. Evening courses must be entirely self-supported.

Mississippi has a similar provision. Late afternoon and evening students are counted by a different formula, and the state provides considerably less money for anything offered after four o'clock. So there is no equity in terms of support from that point of view, either.

Another view of access was developed by Zitzewitz and Alfred at the University of Michigan. By defining student turn-away as the cohort of students who have considered attending a college but never complete any formal coursework, they brought into focus another group that may be a part of the total picture of equal access even though they seldom have been identified.

Zitzewitz and Alfred identified three types of determinants for turn-away students: those which were determined by the prospective student's background, personal family problems, individual time demands, and/or financial resources; those beyond the institution's control that were the product of an immediate environment, such as the availability of financial aid, the existence of competing programs at other institutions, and the availability of jobs themselves (One of the major costs of attending college is the earnings that you must give up in order to attend, and since many people cannot really afford to give up earnings, colleges end up with many part-time students); and those causal factors that result from the individual's interaction with the institution and are subject to control through institutional policies, such as scheduling. Some colleges have found the weekend college very effective. These colleges have classes on Friday night, Saturday, and even Sunday to allow people who can't get there other times of the week to attend. Difficulty completing registration is another dimension. How easy is it to register? There are also difficulties adhering to the tuition payment schedules. Some colleges have gone so far as to allow VISA and Mastercard cards for paying tuition.

Zitzewitz and Alfred conclude that colleges concerned about student turn-aways would be well-advised to modify their traditional schedules and to provide considerably better counseling for students, especially in areas related to financial aid. So you see, when we talk about making access equal, colleges have not done nearly as much as we would like to think they have.

That brings us to the real problem: assessment. I'm talking about punitive assessment, because that's what assessment has become in many instances. It is a methodology for punishing students.

Improvement in teaching and learning is really a most important and acceptable reason for using assessment results. Assessing basic skills that enable students to be placed in courses that are appropriate for their own level of competence is another very important and useful purpose. The former is less threatening to the faculty than uses of assessment that are strictly related to accountability. Our current "press-to-test" movement in state after state often arises out of a debate about accountability: Can college graduates read, write, and compute at a level that potential employers expect? We certainly would hope so, and whether our assessment practices are actually finding that out might be the question that should follow.

Are college students learning anything that they need to know or to be able to do, especially at high-cost institutions, or are they just having fun? Are community colleges preparing their students for successful work after transfer? Why do so few Black and Hispanic students complete programs and transfer on to upper-division work? And why is attrition so high at so many colleges and universities? Could attrition be predicted from better assessment practices? Could such practices improve teaching so as to prevent failure on the part of some students?

Assessment that is used to improve the college, to enable it to do a better job in teaching and helping students learn, should be distinguished from assessment for the purpose of making decisions, often punitive decisions, about particular students.

For example, we use assessment in some institutions to tell us whether to admit students or not. If I were going to have an outstanding institution, I would want a very high SAT score for admission so that I would only be taking in those who already had ability. Some have claimed that 90 percent of the students can be taught, 5 percent can learn without help, and 5 percent won't be able to learn anyway. So, I'd just take that 5 percent that can learn without help, and I would have no trouble at all developing a quality college.

One major issue in assessment deals with individual assessment practices. For example, we believe, and we've seen some evidence to indicate this is certainly true, that test items and techniques discriminate unfairly against certain groups of students. Even the Educational Testing Service points out that some of its test items are discriminatory against certain cultural groups.

Test results are often not reliable for placing students in remedial courses or admitting them to special programs, especially within a standard deviation of the cut-off point. It would be great if we had a completely dependable test and we knew exactly where to place students.

But what happens to those students who are on the borderline? Those that could be either here or there are not provided for in most assessment practices.

Some have suggested that students who score within ten or fifteen points on either side of the cut-off score be put in a special group where a faculty member could work with them and make judgments individually about when to move them on to a higher level of activity rather than just putting them arbitrarily into a remedial course and forcing them to stay there until they finish the course.

Test results do not predict ultimate success in college work—even the GRE scores don't do that, yet we worship that score as if it were some God-given number that was sent down from heaven. These misuses of standardized tests cannot be defended because of the diversity of students, curricular variety, faculty teaching environments, institutional missions, and functions. Testing still is misused in an attempt to standardize decision making by placing everyone in the same mold. We may feel that student motivation has more to do with student success than all the testing and standardization that we can imagine.

Why do we need to study outcomes in this assessment process? The assessment of student outcomes has many advocates, yet experience has shown that such assessments often failed to live up to initial expectations about their usefulness. The gap between the promise of the test and the performance of the test often occurs because of unclear or conflicting expectations about the goals and purposes of the research. Careful consideration of the goals of assessment is essential if research methods and measures are to be matched to institutional goals and expectations.

We have two things involved here. First, we have the goals of the assessment process itself: Is the process to punish students, to weed out students, or to improve the program? Secondly, we have the goals of the institution: Is the institution here to educate people or to help those who already have the knowledge achieve a very lucrative job when they finish? Is the purpose of the whole procedure to provide a certain part of our society with opportunities that another part of our society will not have?

The goals of assessment can include establishing accountability for external aid agencies. Assessment can be used to analyze cost-effectiveness. It can evaluate and develop programs. It can even assist in setting goals. It can influence marketing. It can initiate strategic planning.

We have only recently begun to think about entry assessments. Even though assessment in Florida community colleges is focused upon the areas of mathematical computation skills, reading comprehension, English usage, and writing ability, rarely does a single college show success in all four areas. Ramey (1987) concluded that the most common approach in assessing entering students appeared to be in assessment of groups as well as orientation or pre-registration practices. But she came to the final conclusion that scores that were used for placement of students should be researched-based.

Ramey's study was followed by a Florida State University professor's, in which he described what constituted placement and how it could be used for purposes of selection of students—how it could be used for diagnosing their problems and for placing them in a proper course.

Just a year later, we have a statement from the Commissioner of Education contrary to all this research. We're now in the process of establishing cut-off scores on the new CLAST test (College Level Academic Skills Test) that was developed in Florida. We're going to establish cut-off scores at the state level without the benefit of concrete research.

A group of counselors and deans of students developed a set of important questions about state-level achievement scores, such as: Is one result of the required entry testing a decrease in the number of minorities or low-income students attending community colleges? Has the requirement of exit testing at the end of the sophomore year had a chilling effect on enrollment of minority and low-income students in community colleges? Has the requirement of exit testing led to a decline in the number of minority or low-income students who complete associate degrees or achieve upper-division status? Is the CLAST requirement causing students to transfer early in greater numbers?

Looking through the literature, you'll find one study by Helper, who developed a series of criteria that should be used to set up an assessment program. The first criterion was that "multiple and varied measures should be made when you're applying the assessment practice to any particular student." Our scores on national norms are fine. GPA averages are fine. The previous retention rates in the institutions should be considered, and there should be follow-up if you're going to use assessment criteria.

She also said that faculty should be involved in both formative and summative evaluation processes and that "performance-based funding should be part of the enhancement to encourage colleges to do a better job." Suffice it to say that in spite of all this advice, most statewide assessment procedures were put into place without a good research base.

After CLAST had been in operation for several years, we did some studies at the University of Florida, and some of the things we found were very interesting. For example, out of 168 students who earned associate in arts degrees from Florida community colleges and did not pass the CLAST (before it was required for admission to upper division), 49 percent graduated with a 2.0 GPA or higher and about half of those attained a 3.0 average and went on to graduate school.

Here are students who would have been eliminated from further education if the CLAST had been in effect, but nobody paid much attention to that research either. We've been constantly increasing the scores required on the CLAST test, and in 1989 the cut-off scores went up again.

In spite of the fact we've been saying, "These people who take the CLAST test, if permitted to continue, will be successful in obtaining a baccalaureate degree." What it really amounts to is that CLAST is just not a good predictor.

We've said that CLAST is punitive, particularly against minority students, both Hispanics and Blacks. Even though we advised that if higher 1989 cut-off scores on CLAST were put into effect, the percentage of students that would pass would drop by 20 to 30 percent, the State Board of Education did it anyway.

The recent headline in the newspapers is, "1989 Standards Rise, Passing Rate Drops." How about that? The Commissioner of Education made the statement the other day that she thought that since too many people had not passed the CLAST test and cannot enter the junior-level at the university, we ought to do some study about that.

I started to call her up and tell her we already had the figures. You can see that I'm very much concerned about using assessment as a punitive measure against individual students. We need a great deal more research evidence to indicate that test scores are really effective in raising standards.

I cannot understand the purpose of a testing program that eliminates people from further opportunity. And that's what CLAST does.

The CLAST program was originally put into effect to identify the kinds of opportunities, the kinds of knowledge, and the kinds of skills that people should have to prepare them for upper-division work. This might work out very well if you don't set the levels beyond everyone's capacities.

However, when we began to implement the program, we implemented it on a normative basis, and so by using the normative basis, somebody has to fail. We've got a curve here, and some people are on this part of the curve, and some are on that part of the curve, and wherever you set that line for failure, somebody has to fail. The purpose of a normative distribution is to determine who's in each category. If we had left it at the criterion basis, we would have been a lot better off and it would have made a lot more sense in terms of long-range individual improvement.

We cannot expect to serve the diversity of students in community colleges unless we have an assessment program that will take in a major consideration like diversity. Research must be the basis for making decisions, not conventional wisdom.

James L. Wattenbarger is Distinguished Service professor and director, Institute of Higher Education at the University of Florida in Gainesville, Florida.

CHAPTER SEVENTEEN

Urban Community Colleges

By Ron Temple

W HAT KIND OF environment are American community colleges dealing with, especially urban colleges? What are the issues? We can probably agree that in many respects America is currently in a crisis environment. Our position as a world leader is being challenged.

I recently served as chair of the AACJC Commission on Urban Community Colleges. The commission is looking very carefully at what is happening in the urban environment and at what urban community colleges are doing and can do to impact on that environment. The commission's recent publication, *Who Cares About the Inner City?*, looks at successful programs in urban community colleges around the country. We're not suggesting that anyone is in fact winning the battle in terms of dealing with the problems of urban America, but some programs are positively impacting urban communities. The Urban Commission recently published another study that looks at minorities in the areas of math and science, where there is also a major crisis.

The first thing we must do is identify the crisis of urban America. Think back to the reigns of the Greeks, the Romans, the Chinese, and the British empires in terms of the length of time they reigned as major powers. Also, think about what has happened to America in the post-World War II period. You begin to understand where we are and the challenge we face if we are going to cause reversals in some of the patterns.

Much of my career has been spent attempting to understand and respond to the challenges of the big cities. My colleagues and I have been involved in Detroit, Chicago, Cincinnati, New York, Los Angeles, and a number of other large cities. In my world, thirteen- and fourteen-year-old girls are already on the road to motherhood. The drop-out rate in our urban public school systems ranges from 40 to 70 percent. Seventy percent of our Black college freshmen are women because most of our young Black men have already dropped out of high school. That's the world we are living in now in America's urban centers.

Black men, an endangered species, constitute 6 percent of the population, yet they make up 50 percent of our inmates. Cities such as Detroit, Washington, Miami, and Los Angeles compete for the dubious title of murder capital of the world.

Let's look at the cost of education versus the cost of sending the average person to prison. The yearly cost per prisoner in Michigan ranges from $24,000 to $32,000. You could send your son or daughter to Harvard for that amount of money.

The cost of sending someone to a community college, including all state, local, and student support, is about $4,200. These are very dramatic figures. The cost of prison averages at least six times more than the cost of going to a community college. There is something wrong when our society spends more on prisons than education.

It seems that if we really want to have some impact on our country, particularly our cities, we have to begin to spend money at the front end of the system. Sixty percent of the state and federal prisoners become repeat offenders within three years of being released, and 82 percent of the prisoners are high school drop-outs. A front-end infusion of dollars is critical.

We know, for example, as early as the fourth grade who the typical high school drop-out will be. We have a profile with 90 percent predictability. But, despite what we know, we do nothing.

In my travels to the largest cities of America, I see few models of how large urban communities should be governed. Instead, I see cities being consumed by pushers of crack cocaine, PCP, and an alphabet soup of other drugs. I see a government asking our young people to "just say no." I see babies having babies, and I see headlines such as the one in the *New York Daily News* enlightening us about a pistol-packing pre-schooler.

What major, large, urban school district can anyone cite as an example of a system that is effectively meeting the needs of its communities? It is unacceptable to accept the current situation. It is unacceptable to say that our large, urban institutions cannot be governed. To do so would mean the ultimate loss of an entire generation of Blacks, Hispanics, Asians, and poor White Americans.

Demographers already project that many American cities will consist primarily of minorities in the next thirty to forty years. Can we literally afford to write off half the population without severe consequences? Do we really think it will be possible to maintain a prosperous and thriving suburbia while our large cities descend into ruin? And can those of us with a modicum of economic resources stand by and let those things happen? Of course the answer is no, but, in fact, that is what is happening. Where are the programs? Where are the leaders? Who is mustering the resources to meet these challenges that threaten the very fiber of the nation?

Detroit has the largest Arab-American population outside of the Middle East, a large Appalachian population, and a huge Black and Hispanic population. Detroit was one of the many industrial cities where individuals from all over the world could live and not be able to speak English or read and write. These immigrants and migrants went into our factories and earned middle-class wages—and became middle-class and prosperous.

But today American industry is competing for survival. Now these same factories require very different kinds of skills. Future American workers must be prepared for continuous learning. The work system that we have now is not labor-intensive, it is knowledge-intensive. Therefore, education has to be viewed as an ongoing process. Our students must prepare to meet rapidly changing conditions. The problem with preparing the student in the technology of today is that technology is going to change tomorrow.

We must also prepare our students in the basic skills. I'm aware of a steel company with about 4,000 employees that has asked a college to retrain its entire work force. The problem managers faced as they tried to teach employees the new skills of the steel industry was that the employees could not read the manuals. So they've asked the college to come in and do basic skill training in order for their employees to learn how to learn and how to acquire new skills.

A quality education program must be comprehensive in nature and must prepare students in basic skill areas such as English and math. Our students must also be prepared in the enriching skills of history, economics, and sociology. These are the skills of living.

This nation's lack of performance is being called by some the Preparation Gap. As you look at the educational attainment of the U.S. work force today, 24 percent of the current work force consists of drop-outs, 39 percent are high school graduates, 17 percent have some college, and 20 percent are college graduates.

Then, let's look at the educational requirements of the next ten years. Over 60 percent of the new jobs created are going to require more than a high school diploma. Less than 13 percent of them are going to require less. There is great disparity between the preparation of the current work force and the work force of the future. The gap that exists between what we have now and what we need from future employees is creating a critical crisis in America.

We live in a time when a new generation of leaders is emerging. We hope it will be a generation of leaders who will not tell us what we want to hear, but will have the foresight, the wisdom, and the political will to tell us what we must know. They must work with us to regain control of our cities, our schools, and our street corners. They must help us develop imaginative programs that convince a ten-year-old that his or her future is better assured through education rather than through selling dope.

I'm angry, personally, about what drugs are doing to the country and the insufficient resources being massed to combat the plague. If some foreign enemy had invaded our shores, would we not have mustered our resources? Let me suggest that the enemy has arrived. We need to commit every resource to its destruction.

Where do you find the type of leaders I'm talking about? Where do you find the leaders who dare think new thoughts, who dare to get involved, who are able to challenge corrupt values? Where do you find the leaders who are committed to excellence, who do not accept that our children cannot learn, who do not accept that our streets and homes cannot be made safe, and who do not accept that as a nation we are destined to be second-best?

This commitment to excellence and to the belief that we can be anything we want to be if we're willing to work for it has to be rekindled among our young. We know that true greatness cannot survive in the midst of racism, sexism, and economic exploitation. An environment must be created in which every person has the opportunity to dream and to work to make that dream a reality.

What type of environment produces the type of leadership to which I'm referring? While such leadership can come from many corners, some of our educational institutions have the potential to spawn such leadership and in some instances have already done so. Leadership is beginning to emerge from the community college movement.

I'm concerned that while education attempts to solve its problems, the criminal justice department attempts to solve its problems, the court system attempts to solve its share of problems, and the Department of Social Services attempts to deal with its problems, none of us are coming together to pool our finite resources. No one segment of the public sector can respond effectively alone. One of the areas that needs the full measure of our collective resources is the family.

We know, for example, that children from one-parent households have lower social-emotional development and academic achievement. Students from two-parent families have higher reading comprehension than do students from one-parent families. Low income, generally characteristic of one-parent families, is a factor that heightens the probability of children dropping out of high school. The female head of a household is often less skilled. The father's role, or lack of it, makes a difference in children's behavior. The need for impacting a family is further dramatized by additional research that finds that even though schooling has some intangible effect on student achievement, it is generally not enough to significantly counter the effect of a student's social background.

What that says, in effect, is that educational institutions can have some impact on the student. The bleak fact, however, is that the greater impact is going to come from the family. That is helpful where the family environment is positive, but in urban America most often it is not. In order for us to have more impact on students, we will need to have a greater impact on the family.

As an academician who is also an administrator, I know that the heart of any academic institution is its faculty. I frequently say to my staff that the administration is there to assist the faculty to do their jobs effectively. The faculty is the lifeblood of the institution. The faculty and administration exist in a symbiotic relationship. A good faculty cares about its students. Caring should not be equated with making it easy. The best faculty members will insist on uncompromising excellence and force students to think new thoughts that push them beyond their known limits. That type of faculty prepares you to tackle the hard task of life and to take on those challenges that beg for solutions.

Look at undergraduate enrollment and higher education by race and ethnicity. The picture is not good. Actually, the picture is getting worse. If you look at the trend from 1980 to 1988, you will find fewer minority students in higher educational institutions.

From 1980 to 1984, there was a 2 percent growth across all student categories. White students reflect the average. Among Black students, there was an 11 percent decline. Among Hispanics, there was a 2 percent decline. So the picture is not good in terms of the number of minorities who are in fact pursuing higher education. This situation creates a multitude of problems if minorities someday will be our majorities in urban areas. The fact is they're not going to be prepared to deal with the realities of helping to run this country. We will not have the work force. We will not have the leadership. What is the significance of this for institutions like community colleges and universities in general? What is the significance for urban community colleges and universities?

Let's slice the pie another way. Let's look at Black men who earned baccalaureate degrees from 1977 to 1985; there is an 8 percent decrease. The number who have earned master's degrees has decreased 33 percent. Among Blacks, doctorate degrees earned are down 27 percent. What does that mean to institutions who are out there attempting to recruit minorities into our higher education system? What we're finding, in fact, is that the pool is drying up. They're not there.

There are going to be some major sociological imbalances in our society. Think of the implications of declining numbers of Blacks in the educational process. The pipeline of the Black professional is drying up. The statistics for Hispanics are not very much different.

Urban America is in very, very deep trouble. You can virtually walk up and down the corridors of any urban classroom and know, by the fourth grade, who the drop-outs will be. As part of a group that adopted an elementary school, I learned that 70 percent of its third-grade population were minority boys. The teacher said that by the time the students complete junior high school, 70 percent of the population will be minority girls. Society cannot continue to prosper under these circumstances.

The leader of a major corporation recently expressed concern that he would not hire any more MBAs from the nation's business schools. He needed someone who could think. It was his view that the recent crop of MBAs could only tell him how to spend his money, money that he had already earned. The corporate leader was in effect urging us as a nation to rekindle that old pioneering spirit that made this nation great. It is not just enough to keep dividing up the pie. We must make new pies. We must create new wealth, not just for the fortunate few, but for the many. We must have an environment that allows people to have a chance. We must resurrect the competitive spirit that encourages us to produce the very best product and constantly seek to improve it.

Shouldn't we be frightened and concerned that only one company in America produces televisions, yet there is a television or two or three in almost every home in this country? Also, there is not one company that produces VCRs in America, where the VCR was invented. We no longer construct the ships that must carry our products around the world. Someone else builds those ships, and we rent them.

Somehow we have lost that competitive edge, but it can be and must be regained. We have millions of young people out there who can design and build the radios and VCRs and ships of the world, given the right training and the right incentives. We cannot, as a nation, let these opportunities slip away from us. What we need now more than anything else are ideas. We need thinkers who produce ideas that can get our country back on track. We need ideas about how to address major societal problems, especially those in our urban centers. Ideas of how to win the war against crime and dope and ignorance. We need people who can think.

We must not only think about where we have been, but also where we're going and how we'll get there. It's time to unleash the thinking cap of this nation and come up with creative new solutions to old problems. Education, not training, frees the mind. Education frees the mind and expands our world view. It is time to think about what we really want to be as a nation. The good news is that it's possible. We can revitalize the competitive-but-collaborative spirit that made us a great nation. We can beat the dope dealers and build urban education institutions that work. We can learn to work and live together for a common cause.

Someone will have to think about these problems and think about their solutions. While we think, we must also maintain a value system that provides for the creative and individualistic spirit. The best preparation for this kind of new thought should emerge from many of our urban community colleges. One of the recommendations that the Urban Commission has made is similar to the Morrill Act, which created the nation's land-grant institutions. The commission recommended a comprehensive National Urban Extension Act that will begin to tackle, in a comprehensive way, the problems that we face as a nation.

The crisis is so great that nothing less will do. The challenges in our urban community colleges are challenges that can be won, but not by watching the world go by while Rome is burning. We have to get into the fight because thoughtful action is the only cure for the problems we all face in urban America.

Ron Temple is president of the Community College of Philadelphia, Philadelphia, Pennsylvania.

CHAPTER EIGHTEEN

Thinking Globally

By Richard K. Greenfield

THE ACCELERATING PACE of technological and economic change is continuing to shrink our world at a rate that is difficult for most of us to comprehend. Relative ease of travel and near-instantaneous world telecommunication systems, coupled with the development of an interdependent world economy, have heightened an awareness of the need for mutual appreciation of political, social, and linguistic differences. In turn, these developments have challenged our educational systems to adapt to a "one-world community" environment.

Given the expanding meaning of the term "community," can our colleges any longer ignore the role of international education as an integral facet of our mission?

Despite the reality of world interdependence, it is extremely difficult for the average person to think in global terms, since so much of life is localized. Similarly, community colleges have been concentrating on delivering services to meet the needs of local or regional communities for decades.

But the localized strength of the typical community college is also a weakness. Sometimes it stands as a psychological barrier to expanding the horizons of sponsoring communities, trustees, staff, and students. The need for greater flexibility in the face of population mobility and world economic/ecological/political interdependence must replace the counterproductive emphasis on only responding to local needs. In a very real sense, our village is truly global.

We need to continue to respond locally but to think globally. The experience of studying abroad, for example, is no longer confined to the privileged few in elite, private institutions in the United States. Today, study abroad is only one aspect of a multidimensional effort on the part of many public and private colleges—as well as community colleges—to internationalize the curriculum.

Most practitioners in the field agree that the level of interest in and attention to various facets of international education, such as study abroad, student and faculty exchanges with non-American institutions, foreign technical assistance programs, and intercultural education have expanded at an accelerated pace during the last two decades.

Despite this heightened interest and activity, there is little hard data being collected on a systematic basis, either by colleges or governmental agencies. As a result, information on such obvious items as the number of American students studying abroad is a "guesstimate."

There is a special challenge for community colleges to move from rhetoric and general interest to practical, effective international education programs that are available to more than a few students or an occasional faculty member.

The AACJC Commission on the Future of Community Colleges, in its report, *Building Communities: A Vision for a New Century,* voices a familiar concern:

> We were forced to conclude that Americans remain shockingly ignorant about the heritage of other nations. While some students have a global perspective, the majority, although vaguely concerned, are inadequately informed about the interdependent world in which they live. Students living in the twenty-first century will routinely confront the reality of an interdependent world. Therefore, we strongly urge that the general education sequence provide students with an understanding of cultures other than their own.

Building Communities stresses the need for our technical programs to take the global nature of business and industry into account to avoid the danger of students' skills becoming obsolete.

In the 1950s and 1960s the major foundations and the U.S. government made extensive grants to universities to build area studies programs and to move into technical assistance abroad activities, but practically none of this money went to two-year colleges. For all practical purposes, community colleges were ignored by the government and major publications concerning international education during these two decades.

Global Involvement

Beginning in the 1970s, the horizons of at least some community colleges and the national leadership broadened. Edmund Gleazer, then AACJC president, and others urged community colleges to become involved internationally. In 1971 AACJC established an office of international programs, and in 1976 it established the International/Intercultural Consortium (now the American Council on International Intercultural Education) to serve as a clearinghouse and national focal point in community college international education. The development of regional, statewide, and national consortia to promote one or more facets of international education gave further evidence of the growing interest and activity in the field. This interest and activity became more pronounced in the decade of the '80s.

Currently community colleges can be involved in one or more of any of these facets of international/intercultural education:
- Students' study abroad programs for a semester, intersession, or summer
- Mini-study tours
- Student exchange programs

- Faculty exchange programs
- Organized support programs for foreign students on campus
- Intercultural and area studies courses and programs
- Internationalized liberal arts, humanities, and business curricula
- Campus/community program activities with an international emphasis
- Consultation or support services for foreign institutions or countries, particularly in developing technical programs or community college counterparts
- Staff participation in overseas professional development seminars
- Regional, state, and/or national consortia focused on international education

Various consortia emphasize different aspects of international education. The American Council on International Intercultural Education serves essentially as a clearinghouse of information and as a national forum for international education. There are various state and regional groups that collectively offer study abroad programs for intersession courses overseas as well as summer study/travel programs. Community Colleges for International Development (CCID) is a national group of community colleges stressing technical and development services to underdeveloped (and not-so-underdeveloped) countries.

The College Consortium for International Studies (CCIS), with which I am connected, is unusual in that its 180 member campuses consist of both two-year and four-year public and private institutions. Approximately two-thirds of all CCIS members are community colleges.

CCIS has two basic missions: to provide, through sponsoring member colleges, a wide variety of summer, semester, and academic year study abroad programs for undergraduates; and to provide seven- to ten-day overseas professional development seminars for faculty and staff to stimulate awareness and support for study abroad programs, a greater appreciation of other educational systems and cultural offerings, and greater knowledge about specific international problems and concerns.

To contribute to the field, CCIS has launched a publication series based on these faculty seminars; the first volume, *Vocational and General Education in Western Industrial Societies,* is based on a 1985 seminar in Heidelberg.

An excellent analysis of one of the traditional and dominant activities in international education—student study abroad programs—is presented in Goodwin and Nacht's *Abroad and Beyond: Patterns in American Overseas Education.* Sponsored by the Institute for International Education, it examines the broad range of policies and programs for American students venturing overseas. The authors found a long list of educational, social, institutional, and administrative purposes for study abroad and a variety of ways in which they are carried out. A key point they make is that "Programs of study abroad will almost certainly fail if program goals are not specified carefully and kept clearly in mind by their operators."

Given the egalitarian philosophy of the community college, the historical educational and social goals for overseas study of the finishing school and broadening the pool of the intellectual elite are not of any appeal to us. However, the idea of offering some exposure to a foreign environment for at least some of our students in order to extend horizons and to provide an opportunity for a personal metamorphosis should not be dismissed lightly. The goals of exploration of roots; developing more fluency in a foreign language; using a foreign country as a laboratory for students in art, architecture, international business, and other subjects; and learning from foreign teachers should not be dismissed lightly either.

Anyone who has been involved in advising students interested in studying abroad runs into several misconceptions that students have about study abroad programs. First, many think that you must be fluent in a foreign language in order to study in a nation where the primary language is not English. This may account for the popularity of study abroad programs in the British Isles. This preconception is valid for foreign-language majors and is based upon the historical model of the junior year abroad, but the fact is that many overseas programs include coursework offered in English for students who lack the appropriate language fluency.

The most obvious example of this is where blocs of American students go abroad with faculty from their college or colleges and study in courses parallel to those they would take at home, perhaps with some localized twists. The CCIS programs, except for those in England, Scotland, and Ireland, call for students to study the appropriate language (where progress is typically double the stateside rate) while taking the balance of their courses in English, taught by bilingual native faculty from host institutions. Without such programs, we would disqualify 95 percent of American students due to our woeful track record in foreign language instruction. Of course, students who are proficient in a foreign language can take all of their courses in that language.

Another misconception shared by students is that a semester spent overseas means that you will have to take another semester to make up for the credits that otherwise would have been taken at home. While this may be true for students in highly specialized sequential degree programs, it is generally not true for those studying in the liberal arts, humanities, or business. With proper planning and course selection, as well as prior institutional review of courses, all or almost all of the overseas credits will be applicable to meet degree credit requirements, including electives. In the case of CCIS, the sponsoring colleges issue transcripts to clarify the courses and credits, in addition to the grade reports issued by the foreign host institutions.

Another misconception is that study abroad programs are very expensive. This is not necessarily so, for while some programs are somewhat costly, others are quite inexpensive. Mexico and Latin America programs will cost less than $3,500 per semester for everything, including tuition, room and board, and airfare, while programs in Europe can range from $4,500 to $7,500. In making comparisons, it is important to compare apples with apples—frequently, room, board, transportation, and personal expenses are not calculated when we describe costs for local commuting students.

The International Curriculum

The second major aspect of international education is that of internationalizing the curriculum. Regardless of the motive—competition or cooperation—teaching about the larger world should become a more important part of our educational mission and the mission of all faculty in all fields, not just those that lend themselves naturally to the global approach.

Ideally, our students should be presented with international perspectives in as many areas of their studies as possible, with internationalization as a collegewide effort rather than being confined to a single course or just one or two disciplines. Even without administrative support or encouragement from colleagues, individual faculty members can increase the global dimension of their teaching.

No blueprint or pattern for developing an international thrust exists. Hence, the wise academic administrator should first concentrate on providing support to faculty members who are motivated and who have clearly established skills and credentials in intercultural education. With encouragement, others can gradually be drawn into the effort. Most of us are not drawn to major new initiatives since our plates are pretty full already. Part of the leadership role is to see what lies ahead and plan a response that maximizes an institution's opportunities. The global village is not just a New Age buzzword. It is the framework of the future community. While we endeavor to respond locally, you must indeed think more globally and so must your faculty and students.

Obvious strategies to achieve a more global institutional perspective are the development and use of disciplinary and interdisciplinary modules within existing courses. An entire course syllabus can be revised in this fashion, while the general focus and content of the course can be retained. Beyond this, majors or specializations can be redefined, but this requires a cooperative team effort. At yet a higher level, if the entire core of general education curriculum is being revised and revitalized, the international dimension can be incorporated as part of the educational experience for all students, regardless of their program.

From an institutional point of view, international programs are not money makers—indeed, they cost in terms of administrative and support staff time, travel, etc., but such programs may attract numbers of better students, use the entrepreneurial drives of some faculty members, enhance the employability of the students involved, lead to interinstitutional linkages, and provide opportunities for institutional and staff renewal. Perhaps the overriding reason is a philosophical one—can the community college mission be attuned to reality if it ignores the international dimension in today's world?

Community colleges are faced with a bewildering range of possible activities in international education. An almost paralyzing set of choices faces any college even within the obvious and traditional activity of international programs. Added to normal concerns over diffusion of mission, immediate and long-range costs, and staffing is the possibility of adverse local or state reaction to the concept of community college involvement in programs attuned to more than perceived local, regional, or national needs. Hence, while some community colleges have become very active in international education in a well-planned, adequately staffed, and soundly funded way, many more have given mere lip service to the idea.

For any community college to have a viable and effective international education program, regardless of affiliation with a consortium, it needs:

• A strong commitment by the president and key academic leaders and interested faculty

• A commitment from the board of trustees

• Inclusion of international education in the mission and goals statement of the college

• A process for ongoing involvement of faculty and staff

• An adequate structure to administer programs and resources, with qualified, knowledgeable personnel, including a full-time director of international education or at least a faculty member with substantial release time, a visible office, clerical support, and funds for publicity, program development, and travel

• A good public information system to keep internal and external publics aware of programs and activities

• Participation by community advisory support groups

The evolution of the community college has been marked by many great changes. Some of these changes have brought both praise and criticism. The movement toward a greater international perspective will be no different in terms of the reaction it will receive. We owe it to our students to offer them opportunities for international growth—the kind of growth that comes from a deepening cultural awareness and global literacy.

Richard K. Greenfield is executive director of the College Consortium for International Studies in Yardley, Pennsylvania.

CHAPTER NINETEEN

Information Technology

By Kenneth Rodgers

A S WE STAND today on a threshold in education, I'm reminded of the wildcatters of old, those rugged explorers of the oil industry who are captured in such American novels as Edna Ferber's *Giant*. In my vision for the year 2000, educators are like wildcatters, but the vast resources we are trying to harness are not unexplored oil fields, but the untapped energy of information technology.

Being an unabashed optimist, I believe that information technology can play a very effective role in improving postsecondary education in this nation, particularly in addressing the needs of minority students.

Information technology is the integration of data, voice, graphics, and image. You might ask, "Is information technology a strategic issue? Isn't it really something that belongs in the back office where only technical people worry about it?" I assure you that it's something that every professional should consider. Is it linked to major external trends? Will it help us empower our students to learn better and to meet the new challenges ahead? Will it help us to better relate to students? Will it help the assessment issue? Will it help our faculty to teach better and keep up in their fields? Will it help administrators better accomplish their job responsibilities? The answer to all of these questions is yes.

If we're willing to use the same innovation and commitment that the wildcatter used when he was searching around in the fields during the exploration phase for a place to drill, we can harness this energy to help achieve our vision. It will take an integrated approach, a long-term commitment, and agreement on standards. But, with that, we'll be able to achieve an enormous amount of success.

First, however, we must review some of the major forces acting on community colleges and the ways they can be addressed by more effective use of information technology. There's a major change in the demographics of the traditional college-age cohort and the American population at large. The traditional college-age cohort will be declining through the mid-'90s and then increasing, but the overall population will be leveling off through the middle part of the next century. We already have the numbers of folks that we will have, with some modest expansion. We have to somehow keep an ever-competitive economy and democracy operating on essentially the same number of individuals that we have now.

The make-up of the population, however, will be changing. There will be more people of color and more with diverse social backgrounds. These are challenges that educators must be willing to meet.

An international framework is evolving, and it is affecting and changing the basic structure of work in America. If we go back to our wildcatter, we will find that in the early days of this century he could cross the Southwest plain, and with a little bit of intuition and luck he could find oil. He would then take a small rig and set up.

Today, this process is a very advanced science, often using satellite photography to locate remaining fields. Snooping around and trying to see where there is a likelihood for oil is no longer a simple matter of intuition.

In another simple example, I was in a major brokerage firm in New York one day watching a senior partner and a distributor from Federal Express, a person who drives a truck around and makes deliveries. The distributor had his own computer—a little computer with the same power that mainframe computers had about fifteen years ago. The senior partner had a package he had to absolutely get somewhere, so the distributor used the computer to send electronic mail messages back to the dispatcher. Distributors used to ride bikes to deliver packages. Now they have their own trucks and their own personal computers that are more powerful than professionals had ten years ago.

Times are radically changing. These changes affect all levels and types of college programs—both vocational and transfer.

Another major shift is seen in international competitiveness. In Europe we have the 1992 breaking down of all the economic barriers and creation of a global market within the European context. The changes in Eastern Europe, which no one in their wildest imagination would have thought possible a few years ago, now open up markets that we hadn't even dreamed of before. The countries on the Pacific Rim are evolving to offer another major geographical market in the world. The markets of the United States, Europe, and the Pacific Rim are changing the basis of how we compete.

To use the wildcatter analogy again, in the past the strength of the American economy was based on our vast access to resources and the large market that permitted economies of scale. Now, the development of information technology, in particular information systems, has removed the concept of economies of scale. The ability to shift resources back and forth has made it possible for countries with few natural resources to become economically powerful. Japan has limited natural resources, yet at the moment it has one of the world's strongest economies.

In the future, as a recent MIT study noted, the basis of international competition will be human resources and how they are matched to the productivity and technical resources of the nation. This will hold true throughout most of the structures of our economy.

It's our challenge in education to focus on turning out graduates who are literate in higher-order thinking skills. The quality of the work force is going to be a critical issue for us.

Don Stewart, president of The College Board, says that "the education that used to be for the elite now is for everybody, and our challenge is to figure out how to do that." The Hudson Institute's *Workforce 2000* noted that approximately 60 percent of the jobs in the year 2000 will require some form of postsecondary education. Expectations are that anyone who successfully completes a collegiate program will be gainfully employed and will participate in the benefits of our society. This is a major shift in the structure of American higher education that we've never had before.

The changing structure of work is making it possible for all capable individuals to have successful jobs. Going beyond the basic skills and into a higher-order skill level that ties together math, verbal, and written capabilities is the challenge. In 2000, 60 percent of the jobs will require knowing some algebra. That's a challenge that we've never seen before.

What do all these trends mean in terms of how we're going to compete and how does information technology fit in? For America to compete in the future, we must have a skilled labored force and we must use technology. We must be able to support the expansion of our economy with basically the same number of individuals we have now.

The finite nature of our resources and the demand for higher-level skills from our students changes major relationships within community colleges. The counseling, recruiting, admissions, financial aid, and student services areas become very important. The process of screening, sorting, and sending folks on one path for the rest of their lives becomes one in which we are now identifying, nurturing, and facilitating. We can't afford to waste anyone. The United Negro College Fund slogan, "A mind is a terrible thing to waste," may become the motto of our nation.

How do we encourage this commitment to the American community college movement so that open access ensures a successful educational and work experience? That's the great challenge for the year 2000.

The Use of Information

How will information technology be used by colleges in the year 2000?

The new information systems will be oriented toward empowering individuals as well as institutions. Most of the technology of American higher education in the last few years has empowered the institution. Colleges had to build admissions systems to make admissions decisions. Then financial aid systems followed to allow financial aid people to make financial aid decisions. Then we improved registration, student records processing, student billing, and accounting. Then we got around to automating personnel records and the library.

All of these efforts were really focused on an orientation toward the college's back-office functions. In the 1990s we'll be focusing on empowering individuals as well as institutions.

A second touchstone will be to organize our systems to a student's point of view. This is a radical idea that considers the systems of the administrative apparatus from a student's life cycle. The student's life cycle begins with initial inquiry and includes the whole process of program selection and beyond.

The critical juncture of the life cycle is when the individual, at his or her level of skill, is matched to the institution's particular learning experience that best suits his or her needs at the time. We must do this effectively to counter the terrible drop-out rate, especially among minority students. We must then encourage the individual through the entire learning experience so that he or she can achieve his or her goals. The organization of our systems will be much more holistic than in the past.

The third major characteristic of technology use in the year 2000 will be the integration of various technologies. A good example of integrated technologies is how financial services use the telephone. With a telephone, I can manage a cash management account twenty-four hours a day, seven days a week, anywhere in the world. I can access my checking account, and I can trade funds. This was unheard of ten years ago.

We will be able to do the same thing for students by the end of this decade. They may not be able to consummate admissions, but there will be quite a bit they can do. We will be able to provide them with information when they need it, which will more often than not be during traditional business hours.

Information movement and management will also be oriented toward making decisions broadly throughout the service area. There will also be a distinction between information and a transaction. Every administrative interaction we have with students is a transaction. Technology, by providing us with an easily accessible, large body of knowledge about the student, will allow us to manage these transactions better. Any transaction a college department conducts will then become part of that body of knowledge, allowing the next department to incorporate it in further transactions.

With technology, students will also have access to information so that they can better understand the college and make decisions. We'll be able to complete an administrative transaction like admissions or student billing and provide on-line access to course catalogues, for example. Processing students through the system will mean relating to them in a different way. We'll be serving them instead of them trying to serve us. It's a whole different perspective. This will be more incorporated into the systems that we have by the year 2000.

We will also use technology to remove the constraints of time and space. Since the beginning of time, our quest in the use of tools has been to accomplish this. No matter where people are that we're trying to serve, we want to get the information that they need to them and let them make decisions.

The last major area is one that is the ultimate collaboration of all time: the agreement to submit to national or regional standards for certain types of information. For example, the electronic transcript is being examined across the country. Envision in our relationships with our feeder schools or feeder employers a standard definition of the educational record. We would all have to submit our own particular idiosyncratic way of manipulating data and be willing to form some type of national standard so that we could electronically send and receive transcript information. This would create a nirvana in which students' records are immediately available in recruitment and placement offices, instead of showing up three or four months later, after students have already struggled and dropped out because they were placed in the wrong courses.

We're not going to stem the high drop-out rate until we pull together to get this system to work. Many states are already working on this, and the American Association of Collegiate Registrars and Admissions Officers has a national group working under John Stewart at Miami-Dade Community College, Florida, and others to develop a standard collegiate transcript that can be electronically shared. The Department of Education through the National Center for Educational Statistics has a similar process for the secondary schools, and many schools now accept a standard admission application.

Student Information Life Cycle

So we'll be looking at gearing technology to the life cycle of student information from initial inquiry to graduation, based on the holistic nature of the human experience as opposed to the fractionated, bifurcated, individualistic process that has characterized our information systems formulation for the last few years. I would suggest that we focus on a few key areas.

One is recruitment and outreach providing guidance and counseling to all schools in a service area. Recruitment will include reaching back into high school and middle school, because that's where people make the decision that deals them out. We want to deal them in.

Another area is admissions and financial aid. From there we move toward placement. In the year 2000, placement and instruction will be more interrelated, and technology will allow assessment to be handled through the use of computers with video graphics.

Guidance and counseling information will need to be provided so that individuals can use it. This information changes often and must be delivered in a way that's individualized to the student's needs. Some form of telephone-based service or computer-based service will sort out what works best for students.

Computerized adaptive testing builds upon a real breakthrough and will be in much more use in the latter part of this decade. The psychometric work is finished. What are needed now are the logistics—how to conveniently offer counseling services to individuals in a way that works for them, and how to schedule these services without creating problems.

Using computerized adaptive testing is much more capital-intensive than labor-intensive. The individual can take the assessment test whenever he or she wants. In order to guarantee this, you must have the computing facilities available throughout your service area. This may require a combination of telephone-based service and counseling center service.

Computerized adaptive testing presents equity challenges. The difficulty of the assessment should be determined at the item level and not the instrument level. Assessment is not an accumulation of a number of items in a test. It is a relationship between one individual and a full item bank. It starts out very simply with medium-level questions. Based upon the individual's response, the assessment brackets his or her capability and selects lower- or higher-level questions as student responses dictate. The student never sees the more difficult questions because his or her response pattern didn't allow it. This computerized assessment can be accomplished in about half the time of a paper and pencil test.

Computerized adaptive testing allows you to be more diagnostic. If you and your faculty are willing to validate an instrument like this to the curriculum, then the diagnosis of the student in relation to your curriculum will allow you to properly place everyone so they can begin their learning experiences at the right level.

In the future, we will also see a shift toward the microcomputer. You'll have a microprocessor that will be a super computer by today's standards and will have a telecommunications network that can offer voice, data, and perhaps video. It will also have some form of central processor that can store and forward technology.

You don't have to unravel all your old systems—you can slowly build on what you have and move in increments that are very affordable. The systems will have video output; the quality of the television will be determined by the quality of the monitor, so you can have image and computer graphics. A communications protocol will form the links so you don't have individual PCs floating around everywhere.

The bottom line of all this is that technology will give you a chance to deal with an increasingly diverse student population. To be successful, colleges must work together for the collective good. Agreeing on standards and direction will far exceed the benefits of looking at things from an individual point of view.

What will the action agenda become? I suggest you consider new technologies within the context of your vision for the year 2000. My experience and that of others who have investigated the sustained social change of using information technology is that it takes very strong executive commitment and very strong executive leadership to address the problems of our decade. Our planning activities must include information technology because we are changing human behavior. If staff and decision makers outside the college understand the benefits and the social values of educational equity and equality, I'm confident that they will buy into a vision that they have the opportunity to influence, affect, and form.

The system needs a guiding framework for planning. You probably will need assistance from someone who's professionally trained in these skills. In the planning process diverse groups must communicate and areas of agreement must be documented.

"How in the world are we going to afford all this stuff?" you might ask. In addition to being a visionary, I'm also a line officer responsible for the financing of The College Board. I suggest you seek alliances with local firms. Telephone companies are very interested in supporting these systems. Make sure that the system works for you at a college district. Be clear on what is needed and then go find someone to help you accomplish your vision.

Don't bite off more than you can handle. Break it down to pilot projects. Find one that really addresses an institution's values. Assessment is an issue that we're most concerned about now, so I would suggest that might be a key candidate for a pilot project.

We have great challenges ahead, but we're dealing with one of the most important areas of the human experience—the development of human talent. No democratic nation has ever tried to do what we're trying to do in the next decade. With a strong commitment to harness the power of information technology, I am confident that we will succeed.

Kenneth Rodgers is executive vice president of The College Board in New York City.

Aerospace Education Foundation Study. *America's Next Crisis.* Arlington, Va.: Aerospace Education Foundation, 1989.

Alfred, R.L. "Positioning Alternatives and New Partnerships." In J. Eaton (Ed.), *Colleges of Choice: The Enabling Impact of the Community College.* New York: American Council on Education/Macmillan, 1988.

_____. "The Paradox of Measuring Community College Success." Unpublished paper presented at California Association of Community Colleges Annual Research Conference, 1988.

Alfred, R.L. and Linder, V. *Rhetoric to Reality: Effectiveness in Community Colleges.* Ann Arbor, Mich.: Community College Consortium, 1990.

Allstate Forum on Public Issues. *Labor Force 2000: Corporate America Responds.* Chicago: Allstate Insurance Co., 1989.

American Association of Community and Junior Colleges, Commission on the Future of Community Colleges. *Building Communities: A Vision for a New Century.* Washington, D.C.: American Association of Community and Junior Colleges, 1988.

American Council on Education. *Education for the Common Good: Annual Report 1988.* Washington, D.C.: American Council on Education, 1988.

Astin, A.W. *Achieving Educational Excellence.* San Francisco: Jossey-Bass, 1985.

Bellah, R., et al. *Habits of the Heart: Individualism and Commitment in American Life.* New York: Harper and Row, 1986.

Below, P.L., Morissey, G.L., and Acomb, B.L. *The Executive Guide to Strategic Planning.* San Francisco: Jossey-Bass, 1984.

Burn, B. *Expanding the International Dimension of Higher Education.* San Francisco: Jossey-Bass, 1980.

California State Commission for the Review of the Master Plan. *The Challenge of Change: A Reassessment of the California Community Colleges.* Sacramento: California State Commission, 1986.

Cameron, K.S. "Effectiveness as Paradox: Consensus and Conflict in Conception of Organizational Effectiveness." *Management Science,* 1986, *32,* 539–553.

Carnegie Council on Adolescent Development. *Turning Points: Preparing American Youth for the 21st Century.* New York: Carnegie Corporation, 1989.

Catanzaro, J.L. and Arnold, A.D. *Alternative Funding Sources.* New Directions for Community Colleges, no. 68. San Francisco: Jossey-Bass, 1989.

Commission for Educational Quality, Southern Regional Education Board. *Access to Quality Undergraduate Education in a Two-Year College.* Atlanta: Southern Regional Education Board, 1987.

Commission on Instruction, California Association of Community Colleges. *Mission, Finance, Accountability: A Framework for Improvement.* Sacramento: Community College Press, 1984.

Commission on the Future of the University of Kentucky Community College System. *Community Colleges: Pathway to Kentucky's Future.* Lexington, Kent.: University of Kentucky Publications Bureau, 1989.

The Conference Board. *Evaluating the Company Planning System and the Corporation Planners.* New York: The Conference Board, 1982.

Cope, R.G. *Opportunity from Strength: Strategic Planning Clarified with Case Examples.* ASHE-ERIC Higher Education Report, no 8. Washington, D.C.: Association for the Study of Higher Education, 1987.

Cowart, S.C. *Project Cooperation: A Survey on Using Student Outcomes Measures to Assess Institutional Effectiveness.* Iowa City, Iowa: The American College Testing Program, 1990.

Deegan, W.L., Tillery, D., and Associates. *Reviewing the American Community College.* San Francisco: Jossey-Bass, 1985.

Delaino, G.T. *1989 CLAST Standards and State Universities System Performance.* Gainesville, Fla.: Inter-institutional Research Council, 1987.

DeLoughry, T.J. "Failure of Colleges to Teach Computer Ethics Is Called Oversight With Potentially Catastrophic Consequences," *Chronicle of Higher Education,* Feb. 24, 1988, pp. 15, 18.

Drucker, P.F. *Managing for Results.* New York: Harper and Row, 1964.

____. *Managing in Turbulent Times.* New York: Harper and Row, 1980.

Education Commission of the States. "Transforming the State Role in Undergraduate Education: Time for a Different View." *The News,* California Association of Community Colleges, 1986, *32*(1), pp. 4–9.

Emerson, R.M. "Power-dependence Relations." *American Sociological Review,* 1962, *27,* pp. 32–41.

Gaff, J. *Toward Faculty Renewal.* San Francisco: Jossey-Bass, 1975.

Gollattscheck, J., Harlacher, E.L., Roberts, E., and Wygal, B. *College Leadership for Community Renewal.* San Francisco: Jossey-Bass, 1976.

Goodwin, C.D. and Nacht, N. *Abroad and Beyond: Patterns in American Overseas Education.* New York: Institute of International Education, 1989.

Helper, D. Personal correspondence to James Wattenbarger, 1988.

Henderson, L.N. *Application of the Theory of Incrementalism to Statuary Changes in the Open-door Philosophy of Florida's Community Colleges.* Dissertation, University of Florida, 1981.

Hess, G. "Internationalizing the Community College." In T.M. Ponce (Ed.), *Intercultural Education in the Two-Year College: A Handbook for Change.* Washington, D.C.: American Association of Community and Junior Colleges, 1976.

_____. *Freshmen and Sophomores Abroad: Community Colleges and Overseas Academic Programs.* New York: Teachers College Press, 1982.

Hickman, C. and Silva, M. *Creating Excellence: Managing Corporate Culture, Strategy, and Change in a New Age.* New York: Plume, 1984

Hooks, W.M. and Kelley, S. *The Effective Linkage of Planning and Resource Development: A Process That Works.* Resource Paper No. 43, Valencia Community College, Orlando, Fla., May 1990.

Huber, G.P. "The Nature and Design of Postindustrial Organizations." *Management Science,* 1984, *30,* pp. 928–951.

Hyde, W. *A New Look at Community College Access.* Denver: Education Commission of the States, 1982.

Israel, C.A., McKenney, J.F., and Wartgow, J.F. "Community Colleges: A Competitive Edge for Economic Development." *Economic Development Review,* Summer 1987, pp. 19–23.

Jackson, J.H. and Morgan, C.P. *Organization Theory: A Macro Perspective for Management.* Englewood Cliffs, N.J.: Prentice-Hall, 1978.

Joint Committee for the Review of the Master Plan for Higher Education. *California Faces. . .California's Future: Education for Citizenship in a Multicultural Democracy.* Sacramento: Joint Committee for the Review of the Master Plan for Higher Education, 1989.

Katy, D. and Kahn, R. *The Social Psychology of Organizations.* New York: John Wiley and Sons, 1978.

Keller, G. *Academic Strategy: The Management Revolution in American Higher Education.* Baltimore: Johns Hopkins University Press, 1983.

Kotter, J.P. *A Force for Change: How Leadership Differs from Management.* New York: The Free Press, 1990.

Lanford, H.W. *Systems Management: Planning and Control.* Port Washington, N.Y.: National University Publications, 1981.

Lauenstein, M.C. *What's Your Game Plan?* Homewood, Ill.: Dow Jones-Irwin, 1986.

Levine, A. and Associates. *Shaping Higher Education's Future.* San Francisco: Jossey-Bass, 1989.

Lippitt, G.L. and Schmidt, W.H. "Crisis in a Developing Organization." *Harvard Business Review,* 1967, *45*(6), p. 103.

McDonald, J.O. *Management Without Tears.* Chicago: Crain Books, 1981.

McDowell, R.W. and Lindner, W.K. "A Case for Commercial Development of College Property." *New Directions for Community Colleges,* no. 68. San Francisco: Jossey-Bass, 1989.

Midlands Technical College. *Vision for Excellence.* Columbia, S.C.: Midlands Technical College, 1988.

Mintzberg, H. *The Structuring of Organizations.* Englewood Cliffs, N.J.: Prentice-Hall, Inc., 1979.

Naisbitt, J. *Megatrends: Ten New Directions Transforming Our Lives*. New York: Warner Books, Inc., 1982.

Naisbitt, J. and Aburdene, P. *Megatrends 2000: Ten New Directions for the 1990s*. New York: William Morrow and Company, 1990.

National Commission on Excellence in Education. *A Nation At Risk*. Washington, D.C.: National Commission on Excellence in Education, 1983.

Newman, F. *Higher Education and the American Resurgence*. Princeton, N.J.: Carnegie Foundation for the Advancement of Teaching, 1985.

Nickens, J., et al. *CLAST Scores and Grades of Community College Transfer Students in the State Universities*. Gainesville, Fla.: Inter-institutional Research Council, 1984.

Nickens, J.M. *Profile of College Students who Repeatedly Fail a CLAST Subtest*. Gainesville, Fla.: Institute of Higher Education, 1989.

Ottinger, C.A. (Ed.). *Higher Education Today*. Washington, D.C.: American Council on Education, 1989.

Owen, D. "1983: The Last Days of ETS." *Harpers*, 1983, *266*, pp. 21–37.

Parnell, D. *Dateline 2000: The New Higher Education Agenda*. Washington, D.C.: The Community College Press, 1990.

Parsons, M.J. *Back to Basics: Planning*. New York: Facts on File Publications, 1985.

Peters, T. *Thriving on Chaos*. New York: Alfred A. Knopf, 1987.

Peters, T.J. and Waterman, R.H. Jr. *In Search of Excellence: Lessons from America's Best-Run Companies*. New York: Harper & Row, 1982.

Ponitz, D.H. "Building Communities: A New Vision for a New Century." *Community, Technical, and Junior College Journal*, 1988, *59*(1), p. 6.

Ramey, L. *Survey of Entering Student Assessment Procedures*. Term paper, Institute of Higher Education, University of Florida, 1981.

Roueche, J.E. and Baker, G.A. III. *Access and Excellence: The Open-Door College*. Washington, D.C.: Community College Press, 1987.

Roueche, J.E., Baker, G.A. III, and Rose, R.R. *Shared Vision: Transformational Leadership in American Community Colleges*. Washington, D.C.: Community College Press, 1989.

Southern Governors Association. *Cornerstone of Competition: International Education. The Report of the Southern Governors Association Advisory Council on International Education*. Washington, D.C.: Southern Governors Association, 1986.

Steiner, G. *Strategic Planning: What Every Manager Must Know*. New York: Macmillan and Company, 1979.

Study Group on the Conditions of Excellence in American Higher Education. *Involvement in Learning: Realizing the Potential of American Higher Education*. Washington, D.C.: National Institute of Education, 1984.

Task Force on Higher Education and the Schools, Southern Regional Education Board. *Meeting the Need for Quality: Action in the South*. Atlanta: Southern Regional Education Board, 1985.

Tonkin, H., and Edwards, L. "The World in the Curriculum: Curricular Strategies for the 21st Century." *Education and the World View, II.* New Rochelle, N.Y.: Change Magazine Press, 1981.

United Way of America. *What Lies Ahead: Countdown to the 21st Century.* Alexandria, Va.: United Way of America, 1989.

Valencia Community College. *Valencia Community College Strategic Plan.* Orlando, Fla.: Valencia Community College, 1990.

Vaughan, G.B. and Associates. *Issues for Community College Leaders in a New Era.* San Francisco: Jossey-Bass, 1983.

Waterman, R.H. Jr. *The Renewal Factor.* New York: Bantam Books, 1987.

Wattenbarger, J.L., Haynes, F.T., and Smith, A. III. "Coping with Complexity: Another Viewpoint for Community Colleges." *Community College Review,* 1982, *10*(2), pp. 3–11.

Weinstein, J.L. "Eckerd Ethics Students Showing They Have Hope." *St. Petersburg Times,* Nov. 30, 1988, p. 3.

Zitzewitz, B. and Alfred, R. "The Paradox of the Open Door: Student Turnaway in the Community College." *Community College Journal for Research and Planning,* 1983, *3*(1), 5–14.

Dan Angel has served as president of Austin Community College in Texas since 1985. Previously, he served as president of Citrus College and Imperial Valley College in California. In 1984 the Citrus College Trustees named the computer center in his honor.

A three-term member of the Michigan Legislature, he served as special assistant to U.S. Senator Robert P. Griffin in Washington, D.C. Appointed to the American Council on Education's Commission on Minorities in Higher Education, Angel's extensive service on boards includes terms on the COMBASE Executive Committee, Michigan's Higher Education Assistance Authority, the California Association of Community Colleges Board of Directors, the Board of Directors of the Texas Public Community and Junior College Association, and the Southern California Community College Chief Executive Officers Association.

The author of two books and three dozen articles, he earned bachelor's and master's degrees in education from Wayne State University and was awarded a doctorate in communications from Purdue University.

Mike DeVault has been with Austin Community College since 1976. Currently executive assistant to the president, he has also served the college as an instructor of business management, counselor, placement/follow-up officer, and director of off-campus operations. He has taught in several public school systems and was a visiting associate professor of higher education administration at the University of Nebraska.

He has served as a member of the Texas Higher Education Coordinating Board Advisory Committee on Community College Annexation and the Advisory Committee to the College of Education at Texas A&M University. He is a founding member of the State Advisory Board for the Texas Student Information System, which bears his name. His numerous awards and honors include recognition from the Texas Association of Chicanos in Higher Education for founding the Amado Pena Jr. Endowed Scholarship Fund for Hispanic Students. He has been twice honored by the National Council for Marketing and Public Relations.

He earned his bachelor's degree in management at St. Edwards University, a master's degree in counseling psychology at Our Lady of the Lake University, and a doctorate in educational administration from Texas A&M University.